The Legendary Earl Manigault!

"This is a book which every high school and perhaps junior high school student should read."
— *Newark Star Ledger*

"A tough, streetwise novel packed with an important message for young readers, *Double Dunk* is both a harsh look at the drug problem in the United States and an inspiring story of one man's ability to overcome the problem."
— *Ambassador Andrew Young*

Also by Barry Beckham

Runner Mack
My Main Mother

The Black Student's Guide to Colleges
The Black Student's Guide to Scholarships
The College Selection Workbook

DOUBLE DUNK

Originally published in the United States by Holloway House, 1980
Published by Beckham House Publishers, Inc., 1993

This edition published in the United States by
Beckham Publications Group, Inc., 2005
PO Box 4066, Silver Spring, MD 20914

ISBN: 0-931761-24-7

10987654321

DOUBLE DUNK

The Story of
Earl "The Goat" Manigault

Barry Beckham

THE **Beckham**
PUBLICATIONS GROUP, INC.
Silver Spring

1

Kids are everywhere. Voices. Bubble gum popping. As you walk in with Ralph and J.J., your heart bangs against your chest when you see all those potential players. They sit, thousands of them, in the bleachers on the other side of the court. You and Ralph and J.J. walk across the mid-court line. You know everyone's eyes are on you and that they are trying to guess how good you three are by looking at the way you and your group walk, tie your sneaks, chew gum. The walk across court is the loneliest you remember. Everyone gets a chance to stare at you, and they know you know they are examining you.

Wait. A few voices, as they finally end the ordeal of marching across the court, sound friendly. A few hands wave. Some of the players-to-be know you by name. You don't know any of them, but the faces seem familiar. You wave back, mutter a "hey," sit down. The coach comes to the mid-court mark, stands in front of you all until your conversations about report cards, sisters and television shows drone down.

He explains the league to you—number of teams, evenings of practice and schedule of games.

"Okay, let's have some drills now," he says, clapping his hands, a whistle flapping against his chest. "Looks like we can divide into two groups of twelve each." You hear his quick instructions on the lay-up.

"Start from the foul line. Okay, let's go."

The coach picks up the ball and steps over to where you stand. Look up at the coach and check him out for the first time. He has a thin mustache and thick eyeglasses. His hair is cut very short so his head shines under the gym lights. His eyes are brown. He stares at you and you feel as if you're being examined.

"Okay, everybody else just sit down for a while." His voice booms over your head. Within seconds you are left at the foul circle with the coach. Everybody else has taken a seat in the bleachers. At first you think the coach has focused on you to embarrass you in front of the other players, and so you fight, clench your fists, to hold back tears.

You play with some confidence this time. The ball feels familiarly tough and controllable and you cut, pass, catch, reverse direction in what you believe is the right way. Balls are bouncing all over the gym; voices admonish, salute. It is a confusion of fun. You would stay in this gym for the rest of your life, shooting and dribbling, immersed in the squeal of sneaks against the shiny gym floor, in the voices begging for a pass, in the tough scent of sweating arms and backs, in this world where you finally mean something.

The other players, including J.J. and Ralph, with whom you walk home that evening, congratulate you. They slap you on your back, rub your head. That the coach spends so much time with you is to them a measure of your good game. You are applauded, made hero of the group. You are silent as the group walks west on One Hundred Thirty-Fifth Street and a few eliminate themselves from the raillery as they reach their respective avenues. Your mind is now elsewhere, ten or fifteen minutes away when you will see Carmen.

Walking alone now, you slap the soles of your sneaks against the sidewalk. Strange, although you like Ralph, you feel uncommonly safe and comfortable alone. You are worth something. People respect you, encourage you, know who Earl Manigault is. You think about this as you turn a corner to make it one more block to Carmen's.

The language is suddenly different in this stretch of the sidewalk. Words, tenorish, quickly falling together to form melodic sentences, fly everywhere. Puerto Ricans. Carmen has the longest shiny black hair you've ever seen. She is speaking in Spanish to a plump man sitting on a stoop. Music, filled with bongos and congas, the accent on the weak beat, dances through the sky. So does the pungency of garlic. Her hair is parted in the middle, both sides with yellow ribbons. Her hands are on her hips. She is copper. Your heart skips away from you and flutters around her. She turns, her eyes sparkle, her tied hair twirling and banging against her cheeks, and she is there at the landing for a moment as if all the world is at her command. She recognizes you and inhales deeply.

"*Buenos noches, Señor Manigault. Que pasa?*"

"Nada," you smile, proud of the Spanish word you know. Sit down on the stoop in front of the man.

"Let's take a walk," she says, grabbing your hand. You can smell the Pond's lotion on her wrists. "How'd it go?"

You try to explain to her, but feel funny. Yet you know soon she will know everything. She has a way of asking, asking, asking. She'll know the whole story soon—everything.

"Uh," you say, "you don't sound like a twelve-year-old. You know too much." You both giggle.

Even when she knocks on your door early each morning to walk you to school, you are speechless. For blocks you walk silently, the force of the cool, early morning air making you dopey. Soon she starts chattering—just as she speaks this evening without hesitation between sentences—and it occurs to you that you are awake and alive walking down the street with Carmen.

The excitement of her company, of her interest in you and her beauty attracts you to Carmen for the entire school year. And you two are still together the next year.

At William I. Ettinger Junior High School farther east, Madison Avenue, you discover that all of your friends from grade school have been assigned there too. As you sit with Carmen in the auditorium on the first day and half-listen to the principal's message about good citizenship and preparing for the future, you look around to notice the shiny-faced features of all your former fifth and sixth-grade fellows. They jump up in their seats and wave at each other. Carmen frowns at you. You see little Lennie who has just returned from serving a month for shoplifting. "Hey, Lennie, over here, man." A tooth is missing as he smiles. Fat Chubmo ("Chubmo, when you gon' lose some weight?" they always ask) waves his fists.

You try out for the team but don't make it, and learn to dislike school as much as your friends do. The first year in junior high school is a long series of playing hooky, attending parties, riding the subway, hanging out, going to the movies and to the Apollo. You can't wait until June.

Every day all day during the summer you play basketball. Up in the morning to tie your laces after slipping into cut-off jeans and a sweat shirt and draping a towel around your neck. Stalking around for the best game, meeting the best players. You know who they are now, and they know you. You want to play only with the best so you can improve your game. They call you Goat now. At close to six feet, you are tall enough to play with high schoolers.

You discover you can out-jump most of them. Many times you surprise yourself with how high you can jump. You move back to block a shot and find yourself in the air and higher than the shooter himself. Or going for a shot, you jump and feel crazily that for an instant you are much higher than you should be.

One day near the end of the summer before your second year in junior high school, you are sitting on the sidewalk, back against the iron gate, towel around your neck. The game is over. Your team has lost but you know you have played well: three shots in a row from the side. Blocked two shots. Stole the ball three times. You breathe deeply. A group has gone to buy sodas—quart bottles of orange—and it is your turn to take a swig.

Tilting the fat bottle to your lips, you notice from the corner of your eye two girls you have seen around before: Wanda and Zuletta. They stand on the other side of the basket, the sun glossing their hair. The big portable radio to your left blasts:

> *They often call me Speedo but*
> *My real name is Mister Earl ...*

A few dudes practice some dance steps. One dude has his girl pushed against the fence, whispering into her ear. The two girls stare at you. You can see them now only at intervals since a half-court game has begun and the players interrupt your view of the girls. Carmen has not come in the park yet. The girls are telling you they like the way you play and would like to spend some time with you. You think about beckoning for them, but before you can lift your arm two legs step in front of you.

"I'm looking for somebody to wash some windows for me. Would you be interested in making some money: I'll pay you five dollars."

You look, squint up at her. She wears a loose, striped dress. You consider what you can do with the money: buy sneaks. School starts in two weeks. You can't have more than ten windows which should take no longer than five minutes each. You have seen her around the neighborhood—the face, the red bandana around her hair, the shiny shoes. Her voice is high- pitched, young, but grown up; younger than your mother's.

"I don't mind. It's lunch time anyway. Hey, Ralph, I got this gig. Be back in an hour. Tell Carmen to wait for me."

You get up, leave the bottle of soda on the ground while pointing at it and looking at one of the players to indicate he should pick it up. You and the lady walk out the park gate.

"You play every day, don't you?" The garbage trucks are on the street and the banging and scraping of the cans make her words hard to hear. You move closer to her arm.

"Yes ma'am."

"I've seen you around. Your mother works up in the Bronx?"

"She used to. She work in the hotel now."

"She's a nice lady. I talked to her a few times. Boy, I didn't think I'd find anybody to get these windows done before the weekend comes up. Here we are now," she says, turning into the entrance of her apartment building. The front door is open to a long, tiled-floor hall that, you believe, is the basic design for every apartment in New York. "You must plan to be a professional ball player when you grow up, huh?"

"No ma'am." You are stunned. You never think of basketball as more than an activity. Something to do. A way to get together with the fellows. A means of controlling things. Gaining attention. Meaning something. But professional—what is she talking about? The elevator motor clicks as you go to the fifth floor.

The apartment is a long hall with rooms off to the right. The living room is at the end of the hall with windows facing the street and the noise you have just left. She gives you a bucket, cloth and sponges, and comments about how well built you seem. "Are you sure you're twelve?" she asks, but doesn't wait for an answer.

You are thinking about nothing as you splash water on the outside of the window. Basket. A few moves. Carmen. Your motions are automatic, your hands working without thought, your mind elsewhere.

"Are you finished yet?" she breaks through, jumbles the thoughts in your mind.

What's the matter with her? You just got started. You turn to answer, the sponge in your hand. She is standing in the doorway to the bedroom. Her head scarf, dress, shoes are gone. She braces herself in the doorway, her arms forming a V as the hands rest against the mouldings; her head tilted to the side with a smile on her face. Her body is covered with a long, sheer blue nightgown. She is plump. You see her tits. Her stomach hangs over.

"Almost," you say, turning back to the window out of breath and with confusion swimming through your mind. You sense something but your head is too muddled to make sense out of it. She is staring at you, you know, as you clumsily try to wash the upper part of the window. Now you kick the bucket of water. She is a grown woman and you are twelve years old. You have seen the dark fuzz, the snatch of hair between her legs before you turned back around. The feeling between your legs is warm and pleasant. The craziest things happen to you, Goat. She isn't bad looking either. Is she teasing? Find out, go on. This is what you and the fellows be talking about in the park. Now it's here in front of you and you jiving around at the window. It happens, man. You seen it in the movies.

"You still messing with that window, huh?" Her voice is cheerier and still at the doorway behind your back.

"I be finished soon."

"Finish now."

Your head thunders. You turn. Go on, man, don't be afraid. She's a freak. Husband probably left her. Maybe she wants to give you some money. This is New York, not Charleston. Anything goes. You walk toward her. She steps toward you and puts her arms around you. Her head comes to your chest. Your hand moves down the small of her back to her ass. Her breasts are hot against your stomach. Squeeze her around the waist.

"Come to momma," she whispers, backing away now and leading you, pulling your outstretched arms by the fingertips. You hold her in the bedroom. Glance at a row of boys' photographs on the dresser. She giggles and pulls down your pants, she falls to her knees, kisses your stomach, moans, gets up ...takes off your T-shirt...she smells like talcum powder...you fall on her...are afraid to say anything...amazed at the surge of pleasure..."Give it to momma, please...give it to momma..." She blows in your ear..."Give it to me, please..."

"Give it to me. Over here. Give it to me. Hey man, wake up."

"Okay, hold it. We gon' run that play again. 'Smatta wit' you, Goat? You s'posed to cut on that play after you pass to the middle."

You come out of your daze. The phrase, *give it to me,* sends you into a freeze. A player runs by you and shouts like that—something the coach tells you not to do anyway—and your mind goes back to the woman. You hear her whispering in your ear and suddenly you are not on the court anymore but in bed with her. Almost a year after your visit with her, you still recall it. Your friends, surprisingly to you, believe what you told them. You expected them to laugh and call you a liar, but they sit transfixed, listen with amazed, silent looks as you describe her tits, the sweet warmth of her cunt, the lunch she prepares afterward, the photos of all the boys on her dresser the different colors of nightgowns in the closet. Now when you see someone with outstretched arms saying "give it to me," your mind usually blanks. It is the woman lying on the bed and pulling up her gown that you see.

"Let's run it again. Goat, over here. Spider, you take his place."

You never see her any more. You have walked up the street where she lives, tried standing inconspicuously across the street to stare at her window. None of the fellows see her anymore. She must live in the same apartment: she has so much furniture.

"You know why you aren't playing first string? You aren't concentrating on the play."

You start to go up and knock on the door one day. You actually climb the steps (the elevator is *too* slow) to her floor and stand outside her apartment. You want to knock. Your hands sweat. Once you bend your arm to knock. You run down the steps finally.

"See, you aren't listening now even, Goat. You ought to try to get yourself together so you can start next year. You got a good shot but you need practice being consistent. All you have to do is concentrate. You can jump higher than anybody your age. Plus you got good court sense. But you got to stop letting your mind go off."

You will not see her again in life. Why think about her anyway. Can you make the team next year for sure? You'd like to. The girls fall all over the players. But they aren't women with warm stomachs and tits you can squeeze and who call themselves momma. That was protection, something secure. Come to momma, she said.

There is still Carmen. But a distance develops. She becomes more of a friend. She doesn't play hooky practically every day as you and your buddies do as a matter of course. She talks of preparing for college. She frequently uses words you don't understand. You still hold hands. Her giggle sounds shorter, clipped. But you don't have the liberties that the girls hanging around the playground offer you. You will not see the woman again, you know. There is still Carmen.

Concentrate on ball and not women, you tell yourself near the end of the school year. By summer you have pretty much convinced yourself that is what you must do. You want to be on the first, not the second team. You want to start. Tell yourself this all summer as you spend every minute of every day on the courts. The portable radios and the girls. The parties after the games. Running up and down until you think your lungs will drop to your stomach. Leaning against a fence to rest, huffing. Coming back after calling "winners." The heat of July and August smacking you in the face. Being bumped around, punched by opposing players. Vocal, distracting spectators. They know you, and you often play to the satisfaction of the crowd. You know they will shout out, "It's the Goat," when you do something extraordinary.

As if overnight, you feel sensationally capable of playing very, very well. It is a summer that instils all the confidence in yourself you will ever need. You shoot often and rarely miss. You have grown to a few inches under six feet, but come close to dunking the ball with a running start. You feel as if you can do anything. You can *feel* how good you are, and you know you will get better. An explosion has occurred in your mind and in your ability. There is no way you can explain it to yourself. High school players know your name. When you walk into the playground, people greet you as if you are special. Friends buy you sodas and ice cups and ice cream sandwiches. Girls follow you, love to talk with you. Even Carmen is excited.

When school starts for your second year in junior high, you make the team easily. Your size suits you for a guard position, but you can play forward because of your jumping ability. You know when your shots will go in. You have the feel as the ball leaves your fingertips on almost a straight line toward the basket. If the shot is off, your body feels the imbalance.

You become top scorer on the team and average twenty points per game, are leading rebounder. Everyone in the school knows your name. The coach designs plays around you. The other players look up to you, expect you to lead them, and your sense of their respect and your own authority gives you confidence. It is not even half way through the season yet and you are the man. Your passes are quick, unexpected—behind-the-back, bounce between the legs, sudden floating leads. The spectators reward you, and you aren't sure what it is that inspires you to play most—is it the spectator reaction, the loud encouragement showing that a move or pass is definitely appreciated, or is it the personal satisfaction coming from the *feel,* the *sense* that you are doing something extraordinary? You aren't sure. For the time being, you concentrate on playing as well as you can.

One game sticks in your mind—against Watley. You run into the court with the usual butterflies in your stomach. Watley Junior High School is always tough, and this year they are tied with Ettinger for a first place in the league. Your Ettinger classmates have come to the gym early this Friday evening, right after dinner. They are noisy on their side of the home gym. Your entrance with the rest of the team is calculated to psyche-out your opponents: you dunk the ball as you lead the line of players onto the gym.

The Ettinger side of the court erupts. They stand, thrust their fists in the air. They have some foot-stomping, hand-clapping cheers. They outshout the intruders from Watley. Your team swings into lay-up drills. When you get the bounce pass, you turn in a complete circle while dribbling toward the basket and lay the ball up against the backboard—backwards. Again your side of the gym erupts.

"It's the Goat."

"Do it, Goat."

You can't smile. This is serious business. A flashback to the first night in the St. Nicholas gym when you tried the lay-up runs through your mind. You got the shit down now. You have refashioned that simple lay-up into at least a dozen different ways to bank the ball. Confident, a little nervous, you run through the drills and then shoot jumpers from the side.

School has been nothing that day but going through the motions, waiting for the pep rally at ninth period. You rise from your seat to walk to the podium. Someone from the band explodes his mallet against the bass drum. You look out to see a filled auditorium of junior high-schoolers standing, clapping, shouting. Your speech is short; you say that you'll do your best to show who's the baddest. Yells. Drums. The auditorium goes wild again. Shivers down your back and arms. You hustle back, blinded by the excitement, to the row of chairs seating the other players.

You know all the players on the other team. You have seen one this morning on the way to school. As you shoot sets from the corner, you snatch a peek down their side of the court. Avon, shooting from the foul line, is the one you have seen. "We gon' blow y'all off the court," he said. You smiled, said nothing at first, then replied to the disappearing back of Avon, "Well see."

Huddle. You chew gum. At one level of hearing is a coarse, hoarse stream of voices shouting. On a lower, clear level is the coach's voice. Feel them out. Take your time. Don't dribble too much. Remember how to break the press—keep moving.

Slap hands. "Let's go!"

Walk on the court swinging your arms, chewing gum, trying to suppress the cannonball that keeps rising in your stomach. Get ready for the tip. Stance: feet apart, hands on knees, back bent forward. It's to you. Second level of noise—a roar from one side of the court. Dribble down court. Set up. Pass across court. Run your man into a pick. Now free, under the basket by yourself! Lay it in backwards. Ahead by two. Pandemonium. Drums, drums.

Watley comes back. Zoom, zoom, zoom. Passing the ball so swiftly only three players touch it. A jumper from the side. Tied up. Then they steal the in-bounds pass, go ahead by two.

You dribble baseline, then suddenly fire over your head. It's good. Stands are in an uproar. You smile to yourself, tense your lip muscles so the smile doesn't show. The game is one of swapping baskets. Neither team goes ahead by more than four points during the first quarter. You shoot whenever you get the ball. You miss several but most go in. You are constantly in the clear or able to get in the clear. And you shoot.

Strangely, a feeling comes over you just before half-time. At a time-out, you are huddled with the other players around the coach. "Give the ball to Earl," says the coach, and it is just those simple words, that simple statement which becomes a window from which you gaze out. You see that now you are the only person on the court—almost. You are hot and the coach realizes it, wants the team to take advantage of that fact. Now you yourself see your role. You sense the spectators seeing it also. Maybe the Watley players do too.

Back on the court you are looser, at ease completely, knowing now the game is yours. All passes are yours, to you. You play almost in anticipation of the reaction from the spectators. You move as if you're floating, without jerks or sudden changes of speed, but always as if the flow of motion is continuous. Hover around the player who is about to shoot. Wait for the telltale commitment, the jerk of arm that reveals the coming shot, then rise with the player in the air, your hands poised, and finally there are no sounds in the entire gym as you watch him still leaning and rising toward the basket to score. His front knee is lifted almost to your waist. Nobody matters now but the two of you. He has no idea you can block this shot. You haven't even gone as high as you can yet. Your arms move up so your hands are above your head. He's going to try a switch from left to right hand and hopes you'll foul his left hand. A decent move. A very decent move. But you've seen him in the playgrounds. The place will go wild if he makes this shot. Now. Now he switches. You grab the ball right out of his hands, snatch it as if he borrowed it from you and kept it too long. Gimme. Now the gym screams. The ball's in your hand, you're still in the air, he's going down ... wait ... pass it ... pass it for the fast break ... screams ... there's Skeeter running down court ... the crowd is clamoring ... Skeeter is putting the ball against the backboard ... explosion of cheers.

Halftime. The coach looks over his clipboard at the players. "Give Goat the ball." Everybody agrees loudly. You are down by four points, 30–26. You drink orange juice, listen to the instructions: keep the ball moving, tighten up on defense, remember the basic patterns. You have 26 points. You would like to scream, or at least smile. You have scored or assisted on *all* the points.

In the game again, you decide to really pour it on. You start the quarter with a drive between two defenders. You turn sideways suddenly and lay the ball in. The defenders fall against each other; the crowd is wild again. Watley calls time out. You hear the coach ask, "Can't you stop him?"

No. You tell yourself you will not be stopped today. You feel good enough to try new moves. Finding yourself in tight situations, between or surrounded by opposing players, you spin, twist, glide. Your shots are one-handers on the run and two-hand sets from a corner or way out. You block shots with finality, sending them into the stands or just snatching the ball away from the Watley shooter; return to the floor with the ball now in your hands. Your passes slip around and through defenders. You are doing it all.

"Go on, Goat ... Do it, Goat, you the one..." Some yells of encouragement filter through the whistles, screams, hand claps.

At the end, your team has lost by two points. But Watley's side of the court is still screaming out your name. Your face is hot. Your legs are rubbery. You have lost. It's hard for you to accept the congratulations of your teammates. You should have won. The score is 61–59. But your teammates are smacking your back. You have scored 52 of the 59 points. It doesn't sound right when you hear it. A city junior high school record. The crowd makes one collective "Woo" when it's announced.

Just before going into the locker room, you are interrupted by a white student. You recognize him as the editor of the school paper.

"What's your name?"

"I am the Goat," you say, and push through the swinging door not caring if the student has heard.

2

Everybody knows who you are. Here's a dude blocking traffic now, double-parked on Lenox, his brim almost as wide as the inside of his hog. He gets out of the long, pink hog. The door closes with a click.

"Yo, Goat."

"What's up?"

"How you feelin'?" He walks over. Slaps five in the air. Check out Van's vines. He must be pushing, with the ride and the fancy clothes. Ask him.

"Where you getting' all the bread, man? Look at you—you the cleanest thing on the block. Where you cop?"

"McCreedy and Shreiber. I don't buy my boots anywhere else. Downtown, you know. I'm hustlin'. How else you make money in this town? So what you doin' this summer, gettin' ready for Franklin?"

"Yeah, I'm in this tournament." Why is he interested? Why is anybody, everybody interested? You can walk anywhere in Harlem, and *somebody* will know you, stop to talk to you. Just want to rap, see where your head's at, what's up.

"I hope you ain't playing against Scottie."

"Scottie? Who's that?" Don't grin.

"You know who that is. Baddest young boy around, supposed to be. Moves galore. Shoots high in the air, ball goes almost straight up, comes down like this—*swish.* Charlie Scott, that's the man. Can you handle him?"

"I'll try, you know."

"Nigger, you too modest. That's why I like your ugly ass. But you better make first string when you get to Franklin or you may have to leave town. Here, buy yourself a Ford."

Watch him tip, swinging his arms. Adjusts his Panama straw before casing into the Kitty. It says "Coupe" on the side. In your hand is a twenty-dollar bill, just like that. You can't even worry about paying him back. He won't accept it. His way of appreciating your play.

Played against Charlie Scott in junior high. He is bad. But you are getting better every day. You think of the competition this summer at the different locations. Plenty of time to be ready for high school. You *must* make first string when you get to Benjamin Franklin High. The Kennedy Center will be mostly your age, thirteen-fourteen, with some seniors. Everybody knows you there, so you must turn out. Toughest will be the Battlegrounds up at One-Fiftieth and Amsterdam. Some very serious competition on those courts. Of course the Rucker Tournament with teams from junior high to pro. Some talk of Elgin Baylor and maybe Wilt showing up for the pro all-star game. One Thirty-Fifth and Fifth, across from Lenox Terrace, is another monster joint, where anybody might show up for a good run. Then, too, you can find some very official dudes at Foster, One Fifteenth and Lenox.

Van is in his ride now, zooming off in front of a taxicab like he owns the street, shooting down Lenox. Sometimes you wonder what you will do with your life. But it's too tough a consideration to spend much time on. What does anybody do? But not Van's way, whatever he's doing—women, numbers, drugs. You never ask. Somehow he finds you attractive, likes to hang out with the players, drop a few bucks on you. Your mother—no, you don't want to work in a laundry or hotel either. She's saving to go back and buy a house in Charleston. But what *can* you do? School is such a drag. Bullshit science, fucking math, English impossible. Best thing is gym, then they got you climbing ropes and doing silly exercises. Anyway, don't think too much about it. Basketball is something to concentrate on. No money in it, but a thing you can give your all to, earn respectful glances and comments from so many people. You wake up mornings thinking about it, spend all day perfecting a move, shot, then home to dream about it.

Here's a lady now, in her fifties probably, who will stop and chat. She knows who you are. The Goat. Bad dude on the courts of Harlem. Age 14. And they must see that you are kinda nice. You don't hassle anyone. Speak to her, then get up, bouncing in new sneaks bought Saturday night, and this is only the second day you have had a chance to wear them.

Maybe the Battlegrounds. Yeah, that's the place. It's not noon yet, so time enough to get in a few good half-court runs.

Walk up Eighth to Forty-Fifth, then over. Past Bradhurst, then Edgecomb where 409 sits higher than any other building up on the hill. Head toward the playground, your feet moving faster, heart skipping past Convent, the last street before Amsterdam where you turn and can see the Dunbar apartments. People—dozens—have spoken to you, but you can't recall specifics now as you slow down for the last several blocks. They spoke, you spoke, being polite, but your mind was on this.

The ball bouncing. Is there a more beautiful sound anywhere than the tenorish rubber against cement? The rhythm of it tells you what the score is, who's dribbling, what kind of move is being made. Close your eyes. The voices are songs, calling out warnings, scores, picks, assignments. The ball slaps against the metal backboard, slaps against hands, hits the fence, is music too. Enter the yard, lean against the fence for a moment, under the backboard. Listen.

> *My man, my man ... hold it ... pick left ...*
> *no shooter, no shooter ... I got him ...*
> *take shot, go ahead ... watch drive ...*
> *pick up ... hold it, hold it ... switch*
> *off ... move on him ... my man ... off ...*

"Goat, you ready?"

Dennis holds the ball over his head. He takes it out at half-court, faces you while the backs of the other five are darting left and right. He's temporarily holding up the game to see if you want to play.

"I got winners." Most of these guys, like Dennis, are already in high school. Good competition. You can hold up against them or he wouldn't ask you to play. Scan around the park, around the fringes of the fence to see who's here. Early yet, people just arriving. Fill up before you know it. By noontime the place will be packed. You have played the circuit of all the popular courts in Harlem for the past five summers and know who will come when and how long he will stay. Colonial, Mount Morris, St. Nicholas...

Okay, winners. Three dudes you know by face but don't know their names (yet they know yours and call to you) stand with their hands on their hips. They are losers. You know exactly who you want to take out. The dude who's afraid to drive. He stands outside and shoots sixteen-footers. The other two can shoot, and one is the tallest on the court. You point at the long-shot player. He has been looking at you anyway and now walks off the court.

Start out with something to shake them up, make them begin to wonder right away if they don't have too much to handle. Guard your opponent tightly so he can't get off an easy shot. He's not as fresh as you anyway, will want to pass off and rest. He turns his back to you and moves sideways toward the key. You catch the rhythm of the bouncing ball. After the third, fourth dribble you know exactly when the ball will hit the cement, and it's after it does that you bend, push your right arm between his legs and knock the ball into the hands of your teammate outside, near halfcourt. But you don't stop thinking and have broken for the basket even as your hand reached between his legs. Nobody is near you as the pass speeds toward the basket. The ball spins over your head toward the basket and suddenly the five other figures are standing frozen, arms akimbo in various poses, seeming much farther away than you know them to be. Jump and catch the pass without thinking and while in the air consider not turning around to dunk but instead dropping it in over your head backward. Your wrists bend. You release the ball. You know when your fingers touch the sides of the rim the ball has gone through. You turn to see the ball trickling toward the fence. Backward dunk.

A few voices of appreciation reach your ears. There is the strangest look on the face of the player from whom you stole the ball. You wonder at the unlikeliness of seeing such a fleeting expression, but it is there, bare and almost embarrassing for you. It is a look of awe. He cannot understand how you could conceive and execute a shot like that. He knows already after that one shot that you are on an entirely different level. He knows you can do what you wish and therefore are dangerous.

Next time you take out the ball. Throw it in and run toward the basket, down the middle. Turn at the key, grab the pass. Your man's hands are on your waist. Spin around on one foot. "Do it, Goat," comes from the fence.

Make this move, Goat. It comes to you like that. Try this. Swing the ball over your head, stand upright while faking a drive to the left. Your man commits himself. You move up your left foot and drive to the right. But you are taking only one step. You find yourself rising in the air straining toward the basket to slam the ball in from a standing leap begun at the foul line—an attempt you have never seen before nor even thought of. But no. You aren't high enough. The ball deflects off the rim, goes into the air out of bounds.

When the ball is in play again you realize that your side is way ahead. In fact, you have taken all the shots as someone reminds you of the score. They haven't scored at all. Your face is soaked. Perspiration burns your eyes and crawls along the corners of your mouth. The sun is right over your head. You'd do anything for a drink. Of course there isn't a fountain around—they never have them in the playgrounds.

The remainder of the game goes on like that. You are almost stumbling from the heat and take off your sweatshirt between scores. A decent crowd has lined the sides of the court, the out-of-bounds lines are covered by their toes. Now the encouragements, assessments, disagreements are louder and more frequent from the sidelines. Several babies cry from carriages and strollers. The portable radios all have the same station and Bobby Freeman's "Do You Wanna Dance?" *(Sweet, sweet, all through the night, oh baaby, do you wanna dance?)* comes from all sides.

And suddenly the spirit of it all cancels out the exhaustion. You are renewed. You must show them something. They are here to see theatrics, something rhythmic, something astonishing, some expression of a natural ability loosed spontaneously, something that goes naturally with Bobby Freeman and the dude under the tree who is practicing the bop and the little girl standing under the basket with a fried chicken wing dangling from her fingers and the poor kid wearing plaid wool pants in this August heat because, you know, his parents can't afford to buy him anything else, and the smiling old dude with a gold tooth in the top of his mouth who tilts a paper-wrapped bottle to his lips and the colors of all the clothes and the energy and the *feel* and the sound of the voices. It all hangs together, because of it you feel like a catalyst. They have come to see you, have come to depend upon you to give them some blessed relief, something to take their minds off the hell they may be living.

Head fake to the left, spin in a circle and with your back to him drive sideways to the right, toward baseline. Now swing sideways toward the key again. He almost slips, you reverse direction so quickly. Your teammates move to the other side and now you race down the left side of the key at almost full speed, then accelerate past him as he puts out his hands to guard you. Now you are two steps from the basket. Go into the air. Do something spectacular while you are up there, but first, get up. The ball is held outstretched high over your head, your leading knee is bent, pointed upward and forward. You want to scrape the clouds, escape from everyone and then reappear to score. This is your dance, your expression of style and freedom. They wait for you as you decide how to complete the motion.

Don't slam it through now but bring the ball down past the basket in a swooping arc and continue the circle around again so this time as your hand comes up again in an arc, you dunk the ball. You hang momentarily on the rim.

"Delayed circular dunk!" The announcement screams over the reverberating backboard. And, as if the kid can hardly believe it, he repeats himself, this time stretching out the syllables, "Delaaayed cir-cu-lar dunk! Gotdamn, did you see that mutha-fukah?"

An opponent steals the inbounds pass from one of your teammates and for the first time they move seriously to score. You are back, guarding your man who threatens to take a pass as his teammate drives on the other side of you. You lay your man loose for the pass and let the man with the ball move toward the basket. It looks like an easy lay-up, a giveaway— that's what happens with a stolen ball—and you are too far back from him, *everyone thinks.* Watch for his lead foot to leave the ground to begin his climb into the air. You see he wants to jam the ball rather than make a simple lay-up because the jam might cut down on your spirit a bit, demoralize you. Leaving your man you leap two, from four, five feet away toward the basket as the ball is held up and over the top of the rim by his hand, held there before all the force this man's arm can muster will drive it through the basket. But your hand is right there also, and before he can complete the full force of this motion, your hand has smacked the ball out of his and then slammed it against the backboard. Thunder as the board shivers. Hold the ball against the board for two seconds. You can hear the rejection.

You walk along the baseline, dribbling slowly, your body protecting you against him. Soon he has you boxed in the corner and thinks he can make you throw the bill away. His arms flail and wave in front of your face. You lift your elbows up high and propel the ball on a line toward the basket.

"Game," says someone on the line. You pat your man on the shoulder and push through a few people to get to the fence.

"I'm sittin' this one out," you say, then fall on the cement. Dennis comes over, slaps you on the thigh.

"Nice game, man."

"Okay, thanks."

Other dudes on the court choose up. Two or three balls on the court. Various wild shots being tried. One dude dribbles around, show-timing. All the players from the last fray are now sitting around you. Under the other basket, a man has unfolded a chair, pulls out a newspaper to busy himself before sides are chosen.

Nice game, nice game, yeah, solid, dynamite move, okay thanks, yeah same to you. All the little bullshit goes down. Here comes Patricia and Diane Smith, both got big legs. Both wear white bucks, got their heads wrapped in scarves.

"Earl, you still go with Carmen?"

"Who told you that?" Put your hand over your forehead to shield out the sun. Look at Dennis to one side and Bobby to the other as if they must know the answer.

"You gon' answer the question or ask another?"

"I ain't seen Carmen all summer."

"Don't give us that jive. You took her to Coney Island last Sunday."

"I was playing ball all day Sunday. You know that."

"Hello, *Dennis.* You stopped speaking, huh?"

"I said hello to you when you first came over here, girl. Didn't I, Goat?"

"Them girls ain't nothing but trouble, man. They can't talk without arguing."

"Oh, you think you cute, don't you?"

Look at Diane and her big legs coming out of her tight shorts. "Ya'll girls want some Thunderbird? We gon' get some soon as we cool off a little. I know that's why you hangin' around."

"I don't drink that nasty stuff. Patricia do, though."

"Girl, you stop it!" She pushes Diane on the shoulder. They jab at each other.

Pull out your twenty dollar bill that Van gave you, give it to Dennis.

"Go get some pluck, man." You know he has already spotted the old dude with the gold tooth and will ask him to cop. Dennis scuffles up, slowly winds his way over to the old man who sits on a bench.

"Where'd you get all that money?" Her legs are gigantic. Now she's got her hands on her hips, twisting her ass left and right. The beautiful cleft in her chin. Her eyes are green. Diane, Diane. "You ask too many questions, girl. I keep money." She sucks her teeth, then smiles. Her dimples are deep.

"Goat, nice game. Wha's hapnen' people? Diane, Patricia. Very nice to see you all this fine day. Hey, watch this step." It's Motorman. Always talkin' about going to law school and becoming a diplomat. Nigger can dance his ass off, too. His portable radio is screaming from the ground now that he has set it down to dance. He sings along with Chuck Berry now: "Sweet lil'sixteen ... you know what I mean. Man, they playin' the death out of that cut, you know that? Goat, where'd you get that move from, brother? That turnaround thing you did." He goes in the air with his arms raised and flicks his wrist backward. "Sweet lil' sixteen. Goat, you goin' to Franklin next year, huh? Should be a hip move. You should start, man, I ain't lyin'. Can't nobody in the city move on a man like you do. Ain't that right, Skip?" Skip, leaning against the fence with a towel around his neck, shakes his head.

"No lie. You can't miss, Goat."

Sides are chosen up, play begins. "Hey, watch out girls so 1 can see the game." You wave Diane to the side. You have to stand up, though—the crowd has edged closer to the court and you can't see over the heads.

"Ooh. Unh." They groan at the first play, a blinding fast pass to the inside. They always react with their mouths. As if they have been injured, as if it's pain that makes them groan rather than pleasure. Motorman picks up his radio. It's a Latin by Perez Prado. He starts a cha-cha.

"Who's that nigger, Goat? You see that pass? That nigger need to be watched. Where he from? Oh, you got new sneaks, huh? Damn, that nigger came to play."

Someone else answers from the group. You look around. There must be a half-dozen standing around you.

"He go to Wingate. Play guard."

Motorman keeps it going. "What his name is? Does he start?"

"I don't know."

Someone else: "I hear Wilt may play in the Rucker all-star game."

"Where you hear that shit?"

'Elgin too."

"Goat, is that right?"

You don't know. It's funny. They think you know everything or ought to know. Always want you to be the judge. "I haven't heard," you answer, keeping your eyes on the game.

"Goat, you gon' play another fray or you wanna walk?"

You can't concentrate. Questions, interruptions, decisions. "I don't know. Wait and see what Dennis says. Oh, you smokin' now, huh?" Diane pulls out a Marlboro "Lookin' for cancer, right?"

"Right. It's my cancer bill."

"As long as you know that."

Here comes Dennis strutting with the necks of two green bottles sticking out of a paper bag. He steps around a park bench and is almost falling over. Now comes up the sidewalk and grins. The old dude hustles along, smelling something—probably a taste for helping Dennis cop, you think.

"Motorman, what's happenin'?"

"You. You got the goods?"

Dennis gives you your change, slaps five. Opens one of the bottles. "I'll kill the poison," he says, taking the first swig. Then he gives the old man a tilt of the bottle. His lips are purple and wet and suddenly very large and wide as his tongue goes over them. He cuts right out, warning all to stay away from that pluck.

"Let's go get some competition, Goat. Here, Patricia"

Amazing. Dennis is already in high school. He's asking you to swig with them. What's the other dude's name sitting to your left—Bobby? Another high schooler who can play some ball. Patricia and Diane take swigs. The music is still moving. It's "Patricia" by Perez Prado. Motorman does a cha-cha with Patricia. He tells her he knows Perez personally and that Perez wrote that song just for her. She slaps at him. Some kid dribbles the ball behind his back then loses it. Babies cry. Another moan. The sun moves toward the river, is a scorcher now that you have had several swigs of the wine. Your eyes blur. A moan goes up from the crowd again. One man turns in a circle, slaps one palm against another. You all get up together— Bobby, Dennis, a couple other dudes just hanging out, plus Motorman, Your knees are a little weak, wobbly. The girls giggle.

"Where you wanna go?"

Let's go downtown to Thirty-Fifth Street, okay?"

"Come on, now!" Motorman leads you all across the street. Zip between cars. Slap against the hoods of two with your palms, Motorman stops right in the middle of the street, in front of a car that has slammed on its brakes. He holds up his radio, spreads his legs, mimics the Statue of Liberty, then runs across to the sidewalk. Everybody laughing. Car horns blaring. Then the dude who owns the ball kicks it accidentally and it trickles up the street, rolls under one car about to make a U-turn. Two from the group run up and stop the car, and another crawls under the front of the car and retrieves the ball by sticking his leg under the front.

Diane pinches you as you head east. Pass the bottle. Sweet, lemony taste. Everything is floating. Through the streets. Running red lights and cars. Now through the park where a game is being run. On toward Fifth Avenue after waving to a few you know up on the court. Wind through

Edgecomb and St. Nicholas Park to One Thirty-Fifth, then up there past Harlem Hospital and your heart skips as you reach the court.

A line of people standing on the sidewalk outside the high-fenced courts. Faces pressed against the fence, fingers between the openings. It's almost one-thirty. Must be a lunchtime crowd. Rubber against cement. Balls swish through the nets, voices shout out. Follow—push your way between the people—follow Dennis and Bobby and the others through the gate.

Guys just warming up. They're all huge, too tall. The floating in your head is turning to waves of dizziness. It is really hot. Diane and Patricia go over to the side, find a bench. Nod and exchange greetings—yo, what's happening, hiya doin' and what not. No introduction to those you don't know. These guys all start, you know, for different schools. Tuning up for the big season. Boys High in Brooklyn—the High—is going to be bad as usual. Franklin K. Lane Wingate—don't forget them. What about Commerce and De Witt Clinton? All the bad schools are here.

Looks as if they're about to choose up. Motorman trots around, greeting everybody. You are under the basket, get a rebound, dribble out to the foul line. Smokey and the Miracles are doing "Shop Around" over Motorman's radio, louder now than before. Diane and Patricia lean against the tall wire fence. Dennis talks with some dude in the lane. He stands straddle-legged, his hands stretching the front of his T-shirt. *My momma told me, You better shop around.* You pivot and dribble sideways up to the basket, then turn your back to the basket and dunk the ball, swishing the nets, from a standstill. A couple of dudes give you the eye. You're just about six feet and you dunk the ball. You know they're impressed. The wine still burns your stomach, your eyes move around in your head.

It's choose up time. Go to the line. Your shot goes in—you play for shirts. You see Scottie in line, hadn't noticed him before. Nod, smile. His shot is good, he'll be on skins. Bobby is in the game. Dennis is on your side. The court is larger, so is the crowd. Cement is whiter, cleaner, smoother. Play starts. You're on defense against Scottie. He throws the ball in but you grab it from the air.

"All right. All right now. It's the Goat out there."

Confusion at first. You don't know what to do. Just dribble. Picks are set, scramble. Lots of activity and motion for three-on-three. Chests and arms whiz by. Dribble around. Scottie's hand on your hip. Pass. Run through. "Go through, go through." You are just floating. The wine and the heat are doing a job on you. You are elated and have a fuzzy feeling in your head.

"Pick left. Watch the pick." Move on instinct. You make some shots to loosen up—nothing fancy—and both go in, one a line-drive jumper from the corner. Swing through and around the court as if you are dancing. Ernie K-Doe's "Mother-in-Law" is on the radio. You move to that rhythm. Scottie likes to head fake you, go way up, shoot a high arc. You are floating, pushing through picks over the foul line, keeping your body in front of your man, legs gliding. Slap a shot away—a lay-up. The hands and the ball are right up to the basket before you jump through the air—*in* the air, it feels like—and slam it against the backboard. Not even your man but a forward who drove past his man and thought he was in the clear.

Bodies bump into you from the side, slam into you from the back. Little toe begins to ache, pushing out against the side of your sneak. It's the Shirelles' "This Is Dedicated to the One I Love"—mellow, smooth, easy. You can move to that rhythm, slower, smoother. "Let it go, let it go." Keep your man out of the lane. Try to glide when you move. Go up to the basket like a swan, rising, gliding. Hands, fingers are wet from sweat—wipe them on your backside. "My man, I got him." The crowd goes *ooh* after you rise up, way up into the air and hang there before slamming the ball. "Off to the right." You love to hang up there, going higher and staying longer than anybody else. Game goes like this. Half high you float, you glide. Eyes must be glassy. Move somehow with the rhythm of the music, of the game, of something inside your system. Everything else means nothing, doesn't even exist. Just this game, this movement, this blurry feeling, this tiredness, this bumping and this running.

Then there's a break. The game is over—you have won. Scottie has scored more than you. He will be hell to deal with when school starts. Tired as hell. But you have made some remarkable moves, you know. The people out there said so.

Sit down exhausted. Your heart is settled though, not at all like the earlier feeling that you were going to collapse. You had no breath, your knees were weak. Now the usual idle chit chat—nice game, dynamite move, shit like that. Shake Scottie's hand but you're too tired to stand up. Diane and Patricia come over with big smiles. A bottle of wine is passed. You pass it on. Food is what you need now. The girls will not say anything about the game. That's the way they are.

Struggle to get up now that your feet are in your sneaks. The high has mellowed even with the extra wine in your system, so you feel light still but much more aware of things. The world has cleared up. Calculate the change left from buying the wine. You can take Diane, Patricia and Dennis across the street. Look up to see some of the terraces in Lenox Terrace. Around the corner is the Riverton. You know a girl who lives in the Terrace. She thinks that she's the cat's pajamas. Loves the fact there's a doorman. You almost hate this street because of all the jive profiling. Fucking bank on the corner—Chase Manhattan—wouldn't cash your check. Nigger tellers think they're cute, take forever to wait on you, then run some bullshit about you have no identification. They don't *want* to wait on you. Even the restaurant you will go to is full of it. Everybody looking important with their business suits and dull faces. Jive mother-fuckers. The hell with them. Play your ball as best you can.

"Yo Goat, wait up." It's Rudy. Haven't seen him most of the summer. "Gonna get some grit? Let me hang." His arm goes around your shoulder. He speaks to the others and tells you your game has improved. At this instant you feel like the president with followers. "You heard anything about Wilt playing with the Rucker All-Stars, Goat?"

"Everybody talking' 'bout it. I ain't heard nothing but talk. Say Elgin might show too."

"Yeah."

Lead them in, shiver from the air conditioning. Watch all the stars and co-stars from striver's row. Doctors and lawyers and prostitutes and pimps and hangers-on and all would-be big-timers. You know every one of them by face and some by name. Sit opposite the girls and Rudy. Dennis on your left by the aisle.

Think for an instant about how many different ways there are to make a living in this world. What do you see? Doctors and lawyers—which you can't be, you know that already—and a bunch of niggers who will *never* work hard, never *have* worked hard and cannot, don't even know what work hard means. They're all doing shit under the table, trying to beat the man. That's what it's all about. Who's honest? Who's what? Goat, come on. No honest man can make a living in this world. Unless you are a doctor or lawyer. And who can be a doctor or lawyer unless you're a brain? Sell dope, sell women, push numbers, sell liquor, steal this, steal that. There is no way, Goat. But you don't want to do that shit. But what *can* you do? What your mother does? Work in a hotel and make zip?

Remember that bullshit at commencement at Watley. Stairway to the stars. Some jive white Jew, class president, talking shit about the future and moving onward and upward. Awe man, dry up. Yeah, you *will* move up, all the way up to the top and higher than that if necessary and possible. Is it luck, though? Is it just so simple?

"Yo, Goat. Damn, you in another of those trances, huh?"

"He's always going off like that. We're all ready to order, honey."

"Oh, it's honey now that I'm buying, huh, Diane? Miss, give me the fried chicken platter with greens and potato salad."

"So you don't know anything about Elgin or Wilt showing up, huh?"

"Naw. Where would I hear, Rudy—from Wilt himself? He don't have my phone number."

"Yeah, okay. You hear about Alcindor? He's supposed to be bad as Wilt when he gets out of school. And he ain't but a freshman."

"He pulled out a tree from across the street and chased some nigger up Fifth Avenue."

The girls sit up and back in their seats. You don't react right away although it astonishes you that a man—no, this is a boy—can be that strong. Raising your eyebrows, you lean backward in your seat too. "You mean Lew Alcindor, that real tall, skinny nigger?"

"Goat, don't. Somebody else called him that, kept fucking with him. Lew said, 'Leave me alone.' The dude didn't pay no attention twice. Lew goes and yanks on this tree and the tree comes out of the *ground,* man. Dude gets hysterical when he sees this. Alcindor then threatens to go upside my man's head and runs after him."

Dennis is cracking up. So are the girls. You look at Diane's eyes. Where did she get green eyes? Look at her eyes, then catch her looking at your eyes. Glance away, then look again and you see she is again staring at you. Smile. She smiles, her lips pursing together, the cleft chin twitching. Now she stares upward, at the ceiling, with an index finger on her cleft. The waitress leans between you and Diane to place the plates on the table.

"Whatcha gonna do now, Goat? Hey, where'd you get that name anyway?"

Rudy interrupts. "Niggers fucked up his name. Thought it was nanny goat rather than Manigault. Then they shortened nanny goat to goat. Ain't that right, nanny goat?" Chuckles. Rudy always opening his mouth. Ever since you've known him he's had that gift. Between him and Motorman one could run in politics and be mayor.

It's almost five. You can make one more good run. Some of the college players who work will be coming out in an hour or so. Diane gives you long looks. Maybe she wants you to go to her apartment. Her mother works at night in the hospital. Last time you had your hand inside her panties. But her little brother, Javon, kept coming in the living room. She's followed you all this time and plus you've bought her some grit. You know you can get over.

"So what are you gonna do now, Goat? Y'all wanna come over my house and listen to some music?"

"I'm gonna play some more ball. I think I'll go down to Foster."

"One-Fifteen and Lenox? Yeah, some good runs down there too."

"Let's go, Patricia," says Diane. "Dennis, you wanna come too? Thanks for the dinner, nanny goat. Say hello to Carmen for me." Her jaws are light, you know. She's bent over forward edging her way along and through the booth, Patricia already standing in the aisle.

Watch in silence as Dennis goes out with them. You want to follow. Shouldn't you? No. You need to make first string. You gotta play some more before the sun goes down. Rudy is with you. He knows what it means to you.

"I saw Carmen the other day." Rudy's eyes glimmer. He's sitting beside you and you have to turn to the side to see his face. His fingers drum on the table.

"Yeah, what's she up to?" Don't look too concerned, but you know you can't fool Rudy. The waitress brings two more glasses of water and the check.

"She asked about you. She's working for some brokerage firm for the summer down on Wall Street. She was looking good, too. You know, her long hair and shit."

You know she was looking good. She always looks good. Last time you saw her, she was looking even better than that. But she is different now. What is it? You're not *too* sure. She was in a hurry, but acted as if she wanted to stop and rap with you. That was at the beginning of the summer? Yeah.

"You two had some static, huh?"

"Yeah. She's very serious about getting into banking. Wants to go college, then business school. I'm not serious." Say it as if you wish you could be. Get the sympathy, then feel bad for pulling this on your man. "Let's go down to Fifteenth and check it out."

Rise and go down the aisle to the cashier. Somebody has told you she gives the best head job in New York. How can you tell by looking at her lips? Smile to yourself. Outside, the waves of heat slam into your face and stomach. The high is gone.

Over to Lenox. Then down for twenty blocks. Traffic picking up. Rudy talking, you listening. Get to the court and recognize everybody. A few dudes from college. Somebody says the Big O played somewhere in town today. Big argument—all the time shooting baskets, warming up. What's he doing out here from Cincinnati anyway? Who saw him play? Why wasn't anybody told? You listen, shoot, grab a rebound, say nothing.

Stay there until dark—a good three, four hours. Wine is drunk. Take a break to buy some hamburgers. Quart bottles of orange soda and Pepsi Cola. One full-court game tires out everybody, but you turn out floating in the air to rifle in a shot or to reject somebody's. Whatever Carmen has said doesn't matter for those hours. You have this—she has her banking. There must be something important to everybody, something that pushes you, gives a sense of worth. You feel it, feel something good in one play particularly as you go up with a dude who is supposed to make All-American and just snatch the ball out of his hands and send it down court for a fast break. *Ooh.*

At the end, the red streak over the building now disappearing into a hazy blue and gray, everybody moves in a thousand different directions. Some have cars, some look for tokens. Some throw towels over their shoulders and you know by the big-eyed look they make at the sky that they have the longest way to go by foot.

This is a trudge and a half. Feet hurt, ache, burn, feel worse as you think about them. Rudy signs out with a wave. You gotta do this tomorrow all over again. You think car horns are bellowing and people are yelling and sirens are going off but you are in such a daze you can't really tell, nor do you care.

When you get to the hallway of the hotel, you collapse against the wall. Damn, you realize you forgot your key. Go down to the receptionist's desk.

"Where you been, boy?" Every night you come home at this hour. Same answer. Go down to her room and sit down. She comes in behind you. "Don't put that dirty body on my sofa. Go right in and take a bath. Get those dirty socks off so I can clean them before tomorrow. You be right out there again from sun-up to sun-down tomorrow. Think you on a job or somethin.' I don't know what possess you to go out *every* day *all* day messing around with a ball. Lord, boy, don't you have anything else to do? Why do you do it? Why?"

3

"You heard me call you, girl."

"I did not, Earl. If I had, I would have spoken to you."

"You always running from me, turning the other way every time I see you in the halls."

"That can't be too much since you ain't in school much. But I guess if you're a big-time star on the basketball team, you don't have to come to class like us regular students."

Bitch. She's always coming up with something smart. Beautiful Puerto Rican bitch. You'd like to wring her neck if you didn't dig her so tough.

"Where you goin' Carmen?"

"Up to catch the bus. I'm in a special training program so I get out early. I told you that before. I'm finished after sixth period on Mondays. Where you going, Earl?"

"Got to make a run." Catch up to her. She's wearing leather gloves. Books cradled in her arms. You used to carry them years ago—in junior high, wasn't it? Will she let you put your arm around her? Yes. She's warm. Green suede coat is warm. Gray sky and cold as hell. You hope Romeo's apartment is heated this time. "I'm going to Lex to the subway." All right, say what you want to say, get it out, man, stop jiving. "So you put me down, huh?"

She stops and turns in the January cold. You get a whiff of her Pond's lotion. Her copper face glows although there's no sun. Bright eyes stare at you.

"Of course not. We're still friends."

"Friends—that's all?"

"Well, Earl ... I mean ... we're two different people, you know?"

"No, I don't know. I don't know what you talking about two different people for. We weren't two different people before."

"You're mumbling. I can't hear you."

"You know what I'm saying."

"Earl, I want to get out of here. I decided that a long time ago, when we used to hang out a lot. There's only one way you can do it—get a good job and pay for whatever you want, for whatever it takes for you to feel like a person."

"I want to get out of here too." You feel awkward. Actually you hadn't thought too much about these things. This chick is always talking about something heavy. Get out for what?

"Yeah? That's why you're leaving school at sixth period. Where're you going—to the movies? Or to somebody's house to party? You don't want to leave, Earl, and I'm not going to try to convince you."

"So you put me down because I don't want to leave the ghetto, huh?"

"No, I'm not putting you down at all. I'll always be your friend. We just have two different directions. I can't be your girl friend and think opposite the way you do."

"And what is my direction?"

"You don't have one. Here you are one of the best players in the city as a junior and you don't even know how important it is to be in school."

"Carmen, I don't understand that crap. It's boring. The teachers don't care about you. Students sleep all day in class."

"You can understand if you want to. I have to go. Call me sometime, friend."

Watch her turn away from you and go up One-Sixteenth. She has smiled, has squeezed your hand before turning. Just like in the movies. Just like Carmen to be just like in the movies. Put your hands in your jacket pocket. Walk behind her. Simply wave when you pass her on the corner at Second Avenue. Keep going up to Lexington. That was the finest mamma you have ever known. Now she's just a friend. You know what she's talking about, too. You just can't figure it out. Later, you'll have time. Later.

Down into the subway. It stinks. Somebody pissed, as usual. Look at the bums in gray clothes. Students cutting classes, got the nerve to be carrying books. Old ladies returning from day's work. Spanish, Spanish. One day you'll be able to take cabs. This is crap—dirty, ugliness. Here comes Pelham Bay. Skip under the turnstile while the thunder of the train's entering keeps everybody's attention. Sit, close your eyes.

Mister Giddibout has been talking about simple interest. What kind of shit is that? Somebody has said they simply have no interest. Class cracks up. Even you smile. That was really on time. Principal is interest and something to do with rate. Then Motorman break's in with, "The principal has no interest in our rate of growth." More haha's. That's odd for Motorman. He's usually attentive. Claims he's going to law school.

Get off at One Hundred Sixty-First. Walk down to Jerome and then up that fucking hill. What does principal and interest have to do with your life anyway? You have nothing in the bank. That's the trouble with all of that shit in school anyway. It has nothing to do with your life. Civics. Congress and all those fucking bills. English and those Goddamned compound and complex sentences. When will you ever need any of that shit? How does it apply to your life? Isn't there anything interesting about school? Can't the teachers do anything other than read from a book you have in front of you anyway? Here. This big-assed brick apartment building that looks like a castle. Walk up—you can hear the music from the lobby—to the second landing. Somebody peeks through the hole, lets you in—Romeo himself.

"It's the Goat. Hey, *hombre,* wha's happenen?" His eyes are red. Shake hands. He throws an arm around your shoulder, leads you into the hallway, then the living room off to the right. Place is filled with smoke and spooks. Greetings from everybody. Goat. Goat. What's up Goat? It's the Goat. Hey babee—what know good. What is. What is. Come on in, give me five. What say. What's look like? Un huh. See made it. Lookin' good. All ride. Okay. You got it. How feel, Goat? Everything everything? I see you. How's it goin'? Yeah, come on in. People laid out on large pillows. Glass table in the middle with bags of reefer, wine bottles, glasses, ash trays. Romeo's box is cooking. Who is it—the mellow Shirelles, singing "Soldier Boy." *Oh my little soldier boy. I'll be true to you.* "Cop a squat, Earl. Make self at home. You home, home. You know where everything at"—arms flourishing—"refridge in the back and shit. Got some good brew. Hey, man, you ever hear of this brew from Mexico"—snapping his fingers— " you know, uh ... what the hell's the name of that shit? Hey Caesar, what's the name of that brew—my father brought it for me—we got in the fridge?"

"Hey. I'm dancing, man. Catch me on the rebound."

"Aw you funnytime-looking spook, you call that dancing? Hey Goat, see this chick coming over here now? She been asking about you, man. Why don't you hit on her. She's a senior. Got some nice tits, huh man? Check the wal . . ."

She comes right up to you, walking as if she's about to fall over. One of those big-hip walks where the sister waddles a little. You've seen them going deep into hip bends and twists like walking in a curve. Left, right, left, right. Down on the left, then up to the right.

"Hi ya doin', Goat?"

"Hey, what's happenen?" Put your hand out, reach for the joint. "Let me try this."

"Be careful, it's Colombian. My name is Cindy."

She does have some nice tits. "Yeah, I've seen you around." Nice dark lips—thick. Short hair. Brown eyes moving over your face. She is fine. How do you get these fine women without doing anything? All you do is walk in the door good and she comes after you. Luck ain't the word for it. "Let me take off my jacket. I'll be right back." Romeo takes it for you and you return, this time counting the folk in the room. Must be about twenty—decent size for a hooky party. Direct Cindy over to a pillow.

"I saw the GW game. You played your ass off, never saw anything like that tip-in. The whole place went wild. How'd you even think of something like that, Goat?" Her face tilts toward yours. Joint's gone—you have finished it. The colors suddenly explode: The red carpet, shag—easy to play with by pulling the ends—white and green bean bag pillows. Mellow, very mellow. The walls are clean and white. You smile, then start grinning. Think about that tip-in. Funny as hell going that high in the air. What can you say?

"It just came to me, you know. Something in me said, 'try this.'" Are you making any sense at all? Doesn't sound like it. Your voice seems to be losing you. Your mouth is moving, but are words coming out? Some couples get up to jerk. It's the Contours. *Do you love me (Do you love me?) Do you love me (Do you love me?) Now that I can dance ... I can do the twist ... Do you like it like this?* That's one dance you can do if necessary. Usually you play dead, though, get high, talk to the women.

"Hey, we gon' put on some Latin music. I'm tired of this American b.s." Romeo comes back into the room. This time Wanda is holding his hand.

"Well, whose record is it, anyway? Ain' nobody told you to put on that shit." Some voice from the corner.

"What shit you talking about, man?" Romeo searches through his collection of albums leaning against the wall next to you. "Hey, Goat, I forgot to tell you my little brother wanted to see you. He said he had some shots to show you. Ha ha ha." Nod your head and smile.

"I'm talking about that good shit you got over there you calling American b.s. Gene Chandler, Isley Brothers. You got the Marvelettes, you got Barbara Lynn, you got Shep and the Limelites."

"Well, yeah. But you know what I'm putting on now?— Some real shit. Check this out. This is the man—Johnny Pacheco. This brother gets down. And look who's on deck—Tito Puento and Eddie Palmieri. And don't even talk about Joe Cuba."

The percussion and bass start booming now that Latin has taken over. More joints are rolled, are going around. This is one of those stogies. Your eyelids get heavy. Where were you anyway? Oh yeah, the G.W. game. Look over at Cindy. She's nodding her head to the beat. A lot of people are doing the cha-cha. Romeo is into his thing and saying this reminds him of the Palladium.

Yeah, it was a regular foul shot situation. A one-and-one. You lined up on the far side, close to the foul line. Reese makes the first try and you are just bent over now with your fingers pulling down on the edges of your shorts when the second shot hits the rim and floats in the air, coming down toward the foul line. Something tells you to jump. You glide into the air just a few feet in front of Reese and grab the ball, which is not even rotating, with both hands. And now you are struck with the fascinating idea of jamming the ball from there. You are already in the air and your body is already leaning toward the basket. Why not. Show George Washington what you think of them. Make it clear you mean business. Slam it through the net with enough force to take the air out of their stomachs. Do it. *BLAM.* Leave the ball trickling along the floor, snatch a look at one of the bewildered G. W. cheerleaders. Turn now that your feet are on the floor, bump into a few chests—you don't know whose they are—and head back up court. They must know you're serious now. Place goes mad. Your teammates look at you and nod their heads as you set up defense. God, you want to smile, you feel so good. That's the way you relive it. No other way to explain it. Something that came to you—you took it, it worked. That simple. That is how you explain it.

Who's this dancing upside down? The ceiling has turned red like the rug. Your eyes are dead, they're so heavy. Romeo is spinning and dipping in the middle of the floor. Tito Puento is doing a job. Spanish is thrown all over the place. Voices fade in and out. You haven't the slightest idea what she has been saying. She's looking you right in the eye and so earnestly too, and you haven't the foggiest idea what she's talking about.

". . . Mister Phuck. . ."

The name comes from one of the corner groups—about three or four. The word breaks out of the group as if they had been trying to suppress it, but it escapes and you hear it. Already you are about to crack up. It can't be anybody else but the civics instructor. Oh this is a riot, especially when this dude what's his name—"Hey Cindy, what's this crazy dude's name?"— tells it.

"Frankie? Frankie. I think it's Frankie."

"Yeah man, the dude actually answers. What else is he supposed to do? It's his name, you know."

"Mr. Phuck. That's a shame, Frankie. And teaching civics too."

You think it's a riot and can't possibly stop snickering. Your neck is bent so your chin is glued down to your chest. Oh shit, this is too much the way this dude is going on about Mr. Phuck. It is crazy for a man to be walking around with that name. At least try to change some syllable or consonants or something. But what about all those times you just called him by his name without even thinking.

"Hey, you know what they call his mother?"

"No."

"A motherfucker." Whole place cracks up, even the Latin dancers now bend at their waists with screams. You laugh too, and Cindy's head is on your shoulder. You can feel her body shaking from the laughter. Giddibout and Phuck. What a scream. How come teachers have such crazy names? It's always teachers. The story goes that Phuck tried to change the pronunciation when he first came to teach about two, three years ago. Young dude—ain't been out college that long. Tried to make it sound like *Luke*. Mister Fuke. That just made it funnier. He just called more attention to himself.

Oh, man, that's what's such a groove about these fucking hooky parties. You can really get off. Now tomorrow or the next day you'll have to beat the mailman home. That fucking homeroom bitch, Miss Walker, will send a letter asking for Mrs. Manigault to explain your absence. She had a nerve for a while. For almost all of October she calls in the morning and wakes you up. "Earl? Miss Walker here. Your homeroom teacher. Are you arisen from the bed yet?" What kind of nerve is that *anyway?* You can't even stay in the fucking bed and play hooky. Have you *arisen,* no less.

Then your moms gets on your case. "Why you don't want to go to school?" Seems like she's been asking you the same question for all your life. You've gone through how many schools and she's had only two jobs—

at the laundry and now at the hotel. She's quiet, the eyes are deep and pleading, her hands are folded over her apron. She doesn't raise her voice. When you were little she could make you cry by just sitting and talking to you. "Earl, come here," she would say. "I heard so and so about you. Is it true?" If it was something crazy and you weren't guilty, of course you would sit there and cry. How could she believe something like that? If she caught you red-handed, you would sit there blankly. Wasn't nothing *to* say. She knew you were guilty. She never says anything bad to you. Never has. She listens to every word you say. Every word.

Only once did she whip you.

"Hey Goat, you dancing or not, blood?" Romeo goes in a circle and takes Wanda's hand over his head. He's looking right at you and smiling, then twirls in a circle and takes her by the waist. "This is Rodriguez, in case you were wondering who the brother is. Ooh, ooh, get down."

Just ignore him. Must be his age—what is he, twenty-one?— which allows him to smoke and continue to party. Been going with young Wanda for years now. You—you are almost wasted. Just cool out with Cindy, dig on the music and the motion. Her head is on your shoulder, her hand keeps the beat on your knee. You turn to see her looking at the side of your face. Kiss her on the cheek. She runs her hand along your thigh.

Only once. Oh, how old? Maybe about nine or ten. You had stayed out of school again. She's waiting for you when you come in from the movies. Sitting in the big stuffed chair. "Come here, boy." Oh no, not me. She's going to kill me. Turn around and run out the door. Crying like mad. You'll never do it again. No more hooky. You'll go to school every day. Keep running until some older boys catch you two or three blocks away. They drag you home. "Where you run to?"

"I don't know." You can't even get those words out, you're shaking so badly.

"Don't ever run from me, you hear?"

It's so dark in the room you can barely see her. The voice is quiet, steady. The shoes of the two boys who caught you scrape against the linoleum in back of you. She turns to get a belt from nowhere, nods to the boys to leave, beckons you to come forward.

"Earl, how do you stay in the air, that's what I don't understand. It looks as if you just hang up there." Cindy's voice cracks on *hang*.

She's straightening out now. Maybe she isn't. Maybe she really likes to talk about basketball. That's a nice sweater she's wearing. Feels like mohair. Damn good question. All your life you've been sticking in the air. You love to get up. You don't know how or why, you just go up and stay up. Can there be anyone else in the city who does it as well as you? You've seen them all. You can't think of anybody. Nobody. You know you can out jump any man within six inches of your height. Answer her. "I don't know, I just jump and try to stay up, Cindy."

Commerce High. That was when you really got off. You missed the shot. Damn ball hit the rim. Was that the first time you tried to go over a giant dude? He was about six-eight. You remember precisely. Have twenty-two before the half but they are beating you. Was it Reggie?—yeah, the center. You get the tap at the start of the half. Drive. Reggie hovers. Laying. You are angry, determined to go over his head. He can't stop you, not one person between you and scoring. He's more than a half-foot taller than you. Rise up. You go *over* his head and just miss tipping it in nicely, but you put spin on the ball and it bounces off the rim. You still go completely over him and miss only because of bad placement. He *couldn't* have stopped you.

Well, you're definitely too big to be whipped on now. No way at sixteen can she even think about whipping you for playing hooky. But your moms ain't thinking about hittin' on you anyway. You can count the number of times she's even scolded you. Too bad she doesn't like basketball as much as she does baseball. Wonder how Romeo got into these bean bags? Pretty hip things, but you got to move around in them a lot. They're still more comfortable than chairs. Ain't this a bitch—there ain't a ball player in the room but me. Anyway, they all know me, know who I am.

Chairs. Chairs. You remember the chairs being thrown. Last summer in the high school Rucker Tournament. Hot as hell. Somebody at half time twists the bottom of his jersey and wrings out a cupful of perspiration on the ground. The all-star game. Everybody in Harlem is out there. They have chairs—the folding wood chairs—lined up along the out-of-bounds lines. You can't even dribble along the line, the chairs are so close. Couple of bitches you are hitting on. Carmen is even there for a while. All the bad young boys eager to make a rep for themselves. You are nervous as you warm up and realize that after one year of high school you are considered one of the best. This is the baddest bunch of schoolboy players in the country. This is where it counts—in New York. A few bad dudes come out of Philly and from the coast. But here is where the competition is for real. Alcindor is loping around, getting ready for his second year at Power. Everybody comes to see him, really, towering above the trees, the gum sliding inside his cheek, arms swinging at his sides. Vaughan Harper. "Big Thing" Ed Henry. Val Reed. All the bad boys.

At warm-up Lew stands around the basket and throws in hooks and dunks. Crowd goes "ooh" everytime he jams it. Don't look too concerned about anything, that's the trick: be cool. You check out Alcindor to see how he does it. Motorman is on hand to give unofficial commentary. He knows all the stars—tells the crowd who just shot what, what school the player goes to, how tall, his average, what college he's interested in. Babies cry. You hear somebody's television. WWRL, "Your community station" is on two radios. *Blam, blam, blam*—three dunks in a row. Two kids are in a tree just above a basket. *Swish*—somebody hits from outside. You take off a missed shot and dribble out to the chairs, turn, bank it. One of the kids in the tree pops a firecracker. You go back under the basket. Over the heads of the crowd you see the ice cream man's truck. Behind the hot dog man is the frozen lemonade man, and behind him is the soft pretzel vendor. Here's a dude walking just inside the in-bounds line. He's selling cotton candy.

You think while you're throwing up a lay-up of the dudes you've seen at the Rucker: the Hawk; Big Wilt; Pablo Robinson, who could trick a stadium; Clinton Roberts, who you also hear went on to the Globetrotters; Helicopter, rejector of everything. You feel something about this all-star game. It's the crowd. Middle of the summer. Some outstanding ball is expected. Comments from the crowd. "Hey Jojo, Christine said she ain't gon' give you none if you don't score 30 ... Look out, Big Thing, don't hurt nobody ... Yo Bob, ain't you got no new moves yet?... Man, take that sorry hook on back downtown. You won't score nothing here with that shit." Dudes are serious too. You've seen cats lose their girlfriends on account of bad play. Chicks would just walk away from the game with somebody else.

Game gets started and everybody is running his ass off. You're sure glad Lew is on your team the way he rejects the first shot. Damn frightening the way he simply knocks the shit out of the court and into the street. "Reject that shit with authority!" You know it's Motorman. "You won't try that no more, will you?" Laughter. Run back, set up a play. Glide. Take ball, head fake, dribble to left, pass off. Already you know you can take your man. That wasn't even your quickest fake and his foot was trailing off balance. Next time you'll drive right past him.

You sit half-dazed in the living room of Romeo's, about to sober up, Cindy's hand on your thigh, her nose warm against your neck, and think back to this game and this move. You can see it clearly now. Lew gets a rebound and here it comes. You run down court while looking back. Pass hits you in the stomach right at the top of the key. Three big dudes have fallen back to guard. They are like guards, too-big dudes, over six-eight—with two on either side and one in the middle. Later someone tells you it was Val and Vaughan on both sides, Big Thing in the middle. No time to set up, so keep going straight down the lane. You hear somebody yell, "Behind you," but you won't hardly pass off now. The three stand there, get set to pulverize you. There's no way you can get even close to the basket without them banging you around at least a little. Get strength from somewhere. Feel that you can do anything. Feel lifted by the crowd. Begin your leap. Go up, Goat. Palm the ball, hold it back by your hip. They all go up too. You can't even see the basket, but for a split second it seems that you have gone an inch higher than they, that you are still up there as they begin to fall back to earth. A tangle of wet brown and black faces, arms, palms, chest. It's all arms and hands in front of you, but you are still higher than any of them, so you sling the ball in an arc up from your hip, up to the sky and then finally down through the white cotton strings that are so clean and new for this game. *Blam lam.* The beautiful shaking rumble of the backboard. Noise that everyone understands.

Now come crashing down to the ground, the hard concrete, with the three defenders stumbling and falling over you like the time you were in a play at PS 119 and you all got all mixed up and wound up bumping into each other. Nobody falls here but everybody is off balance. Now the part you remember so clearly and will remember for the rest of your life. Chairs. Chairs are thrown on the court. Scared the hell out of you at first. You don't know what the crashing noise is on the side until you turn to see a chair a few feet away from you, legs folded up. People on the sidelines are throwing chairs on the court because they can think of no other way to show their amazement.

"It is the Goat, ladies and gentlemen. He has done a throwdown on three of the giants on New York and lived to tell about it," shouts Motorman, now having taken over at half-court with a portable megaphone. "Have you ever seen anything like this? History is being made. It's the Goat, ladies and gentlemen. Let the name stick in your minds. The Goat has done it."

They say later the game is stopped for ten minutes. You only recall the hands slapping your back, phrases like "damn nice," "out of sight," "hellified." You can't distinguish any faces, any voices. It's confusion, a beautiful confusion. Jitteriness in your stomach. Chairs. You wonder when was the last time somebody threw chairs on the court. People talk about it for days. Little kids point at you and mention they were there when you did it. "I heard about those chairs," an old lady taking numbers would say. 'Turned out the park, huh?" asks a barber.

"Hey, Romeo, I thought we were going to catch a flick." This comes at the end of a Palimeri. There is only the quiet click of the record player arm moving off the forty-five and you are staring at the wall and fading away from the all-star game. Romeo stops, runs over to click the box off, asks if anyone wants to go downtown to the movies. Everybody yells out *yes.* You are feeling sober now. Cindy looks straight. Okay, let's go. What will be seen? Go downtown and check it out. Always some good monster movie. You can get there by four before all the traffic starts and the subway gets jammed up. Romeo hustles around, Wanda follows him, emptying ashtrays, picking up glasses, kicking a pillow in place. You stretch, look out the window and remember you are in the Bronx, where your moms worked in a laundry for almost a dozen years. You haven't worked a day in your life. Here you are just coming to, having partied your ass off. And will do it twice more this week.

Well, what else is there? You wonder. You know there's something, but what? Now go down the landing to the first floor and wait with the others for Romeo and Wanda. Small talk, giggles. Check that ride. So-and-so was robbed. What's-his-name has some good smoke. Romeo and Wanda meet you all on the sidewalk and the group of you march down the hill toward Jerome Avenue and the downtown express to Forty-Second Street.

4

One day they will have air-conditioned schools and then you will come regularly. You think that's what you'll tell Shanker when you see him. He got to be calling you in because of missed classes. How many? Let's see, you must have been in school for ten days in April. Hell, it was just getting warm—too warm. Who wants to walk up and down some hot gray hallways or sit in the fucking, steaming auditorium serving detention for unexcused absences? This is really a trip. Look at the walls. Smell them. He can't possibly be interested in talking to you about anything else but cutting classes. Only thing else you do is drink wine in the boy's room, and everybody does that. You've been doing that for ages.

There's Bob in a chemistry lab. He told you he was going to school in Long Island. Rudy's going to some place in Ohio. Carmen's going to some Ivy League school. Everybody's checking out at the end of the summer. It'll be all over. Go back and fuck with Bob in lab. No, better not keep shit-head waiting. Make it to the principal's office. Keep down the hall.

Sometimes you think they must plan for you to drink wine and shit, and smoke dope. They can't touch you on dope 'cause you always across the street, out of school. But they make it so easy for you. They must know you drinking wine, halfway screwing chicks, gambling, doing everything in school but learning anything. They got to know.

Walk up to the general office. Same two smiling secretaries, not worth shit.

"Mister Shanker." They know why you're here.

"How are you today, Earl?" Teeth jumping at you. Jive, lying smile. You know she hates you. Scared of you, that's why she is smiling. Always smiling.

"Okay." Don't waste words on this bitch. She'd sell you up the river if she could.

"Mister Shanker is waiting for you. Come right in, Earl." Don't even look at her as she swings the gate to let you into the office on the left. Big, wide desk. He's in the middle.

Sit down. Shanker hasn't looked up yet. Jive rnotherfucker. Scares the shit out of Goldstein. What kind of bullshit is that anyway? All Goldstein said with his bald self is that the principal had got you on something and the principal wanted to see you immediately. Yeah, okay—more bullshit.

"How are you today, Earl?"

Just nod. You want him to get to the point.

"I see the *Daily News* says you are perhaps the best high school player in the city. Did you read last Tuesday's *News, Earl?*"

"Naw. I didn't." Your voice sounds funny. Straighten up.

"'As a senior, he has matured into one of the most imaginative and intelligent schoolboy players in the city.' That's what it says. You must feel very good. I know your mother is very proud of you."

"Yes sir."

"Earl, let me get to the point. You're finished here. You were seen smoking marijuana in the men's room. I'm suspending you for that primarily and additionally for chronic class absences. You're finished at Ben Franklin."

Red. Blank. Red. Nothing. Buzz. Air escapes from your stomach. You can't breathe. Your ears are ringing. You hear bells. Something is holding your lungs so you can't breathe. Stand up. What is this crazy man talking about? Smash his face, his ugly pale face in. Your knees watery. Sit back down. You can't breathe. He's not really sitting there telling you this.

"It's an open and shut case, you see. We have witnesses. We have records."

This jive motherfucker! He can't do this six fucking weeks before graduation! What the fuck does he think this is? You sit down again, in a hurricane of thoughts. The long wide desk is in front of you, ugmo is on the other side and his lips are flicking out words that you don't even hear. His eyes open, close, flit and jerk to the side, stare at you, look up to the ceiling. His hands dance in front of his face. Get your mother in here. She'll straighten this shit out.

". . . I said, would you like to know where we caught you, Earl? In the mens' locker room. We have two students who testify they saw you smoking. You see, you don't have anything to say, do you?"

Goddamn. You *always* smoke across the street under the trees. You ain't *never* smoked in the school. Sure you may have drunk some wine, but never have you or any of your boys smoked in school. He's just lying. And those muthafuckahs are lying too, whoever they are. Why is he doing this to you? Your shoulders are shaking. You don't have a handkerchief. He hands you a box of tissues. Your voice has disappeared as you start choking and trying to get yourself together. Your eyes are burning with tears.

"... Miss Wilson, please send in Mister Goldstein."

Right. He'll explain this shit. Get his homeroom ass in here. He's the one who said that Mister Shanker is waiting. Goldstein must know what the score is. You can't understand why they're trying to fuck with you right before graduation. Your moms will have a fit. You hear Goldstein breathing hard through his nasal problems as he comes and shuts the door and stands behind you. He must have been standing outside the office, the chump.

"Albert," he says. Puts his hand on your shoulder, stands to the side. Your eyes are too glassy to see him, but you know the rough breath laboring through his nose. His white hair or what's left of it is all you can see of his face through the cloud of your tears.

"Tell Earl you saw him smoking reefer, Carl."

Pause. Just long enough to let you know he's lying. He takes just an instant too long. He squeezes your shoulders, then answers: "I'm sorry Earl, but I had to tell Mister Shanker I saw you smoking."

"You see Earl, it's open and shut."

Your stomach is a balloon. Why are they doing this to you? "But there's a way out of this mess, a way out that can be beneficial to all. Earl, have a seat, please. Tell us who's pushing the stuff, Earl, and we'll pretend we never even thought of sending you away without graduating." That's what he wants. "Send for Coach Spangler." He looks right through you as he presses the button. Uncross your legs. Squirm in your chair.

Minutes later you see the coach take a seat in the principal's office. What is this, a parade? Who's next, the chief of detectives?

"Your boy has got to go, coach."

"What's he talking about, Earl?"

"He won't tell us who's pushing marijuana, coach. So he has to be expelled for smoking reefer in the mens' room and for chronic absence."

"You can't kick him out this close to graduation, Albert. Let the kid graduate. You know he won't squeal about something like that."

"I'm tired of this place being the dope capital of New York's school system. This boy here knows everybody in Harlem. He knows who the pushers are, you see? He helps me, I help him. Coach, look, I'm up for promotion soon. I crack this ring and I'll move downtown, you see?"

"Let him go, Albert. He's the best ballplayer in the city. Give him this break."

"Break? Do you know how many classes he's missed since January? He spends more time in the movies than in school. He's got a break by being here today. What's he going to do with a diploma anyway? He isn't ready for college."

"Let him go, Albert."

"I am. I shall let him go. Earl"—he looks right at you—"tell me who's selling this stuff or you can walk right out of my office and not ever be allowed back into Benjamin Franklin High School as a student."

Shake your head no. You ain't no squealer. And you ain't gon' get yourself killed.

"Talk some sense into him, coach. Tell him what to do. You want him to graduate, don't you?"

Coach Spangler looks at you. You look at him, then at the principal, then at Goldstein. You get up from your chair and are stabbed with a pain in your stomach. Out past the secretaries, the swinging gate, the students sitting on benches and waiting to see the principal. Into the hall and all the way down to the lavatory. You make it to a stall and bend over just in time. Open your mouth and stand there bent over, holding your stomach.

"Goat, what's up?"

You hadn't even noticed the dudes in the corner with the bottle of wine. You hear their feet collecting around you.

"Hey Goat, wasn't Wilt the first player to score over four thousand points in a season?"

You don't even place the voice. Don't want to, actually. Back out from the stall, say that Wilt was the first, then pretend you have a stomach ache. Go out holding your stomach, then to the big center doors and out the front. Please, you don't want to see anybody, just get out of here. Walk down to Jefferson Park. That sounds good.

You and Cindy have spent many afternoons in the park this spring. You watch her speak about being an actress. She waves her arms out wide and jumps on the bench. Once a button popped on her blouse while she was fooling around like that. She could hide behind a tree and you wouldn't know for a full minute where she was. She liked to play hide-and-seek. You teased her about being too old to play such games. Everytime you found her she rewarded you with a kiss, a long, searching mack where your fingers crawled inside her blouse and she would close her eyes and hang back her head so her neck, brown and soft, lay waiting for your tongue. She often had to beg you to stop. "People are watching," she would say.

Walking down Pleasant Avenue you think of the times, the many afternoons after school when you and she came down to the park to talk about the games. All those fucking games where you turned out and now they don't want to give you a diploma. Imagine that shit. You really have to admit that shit is low.

What about the game you two used to talk about most—the one against Jefferson two years ago. It was on channel 11, Game of the Week. Your mother didn't believe you were going to be on television. She said that she had to work, couldn't stop work to watch you on television. Good luck, anyway.

You took the rebound—your own man's rebound, but you don't remember exactly who—and made a complete circle while in the air and banked the ball off the side. The explosion of applause almost took the wind out of your stomach. God, it was hard as hell going back on defense and trying not to smile. People seemed to be fighting in the stands there was so much movement. People going crazy, waving their arms, their banners, their scarves, jumping up and down. In the same game with ten seconds left, big Shelley Jackson of the Lord Jeffs comes down the lane threatening to tie the game. You are the only man from Franklin back to guard. Shelley goes up, shoots, or tries to. You float back in the air as if buoyed by some wind, slam the ball against the backboard and it is so quiet during those seconds that the slam echoes throughout the gym. Then the buzzer goes off and the place erupts in the loudest screams you have ever heard.

Afterward, as you are walking out the gym with a half dozen of your boys and they re-live those two moves for you, Bob tells you that the television announcer almost swallowed his microphone when you held Shelley's shot up against the board. "Yeah man," he says, "Marty Glicksman lost his cool completely, Goat. He didn't even know how to describe your shit." Plenty of agreement from the others.

When you get to the park two blocks away you squint at the reflections as the sun flashes off the top of the East River. A thousand cars flying over the FDR Drive. A little farther down the river is one of those sight-seeing boats. You can see the Triborough Bridge, Randalls Island, Queens. Everything is clear, ridiculously clear and bright. This is the nicest day of the week and you should be at somebody's hooky party, but you are in school and what happens? —you get kicked out for some shit you ain't even responsible for. How will you explain this to your moms? She will go mad in her own quiet way. You can't remember anything like this happening to you. No warning, no nothing. Just like that—bam! Out of the clear blue sky. What kind of shit is this, anyway? The reflections are too bright as the sun flashes off the surface of the East River. It blinds you. You wipe your eyes and are doing that when Cindy comes up to you from the rear and puts her arms around your waist and nestles her nose against the back of your neck as she did the day you met her. You cling to the fence and watch the white sun splash on the East River.

You don't say anything, just hold her folded hands, feel the press of her body against your back. And then you can't hold it any longer. You press your forehead against the triangles of metal fence and start crying. She holds you tighter.

"I'll get them for this," you say, turning to hold Cindy and to put your face against her cheek. "Those bastards."

"Tell me what happened, baby. Tell me what happened."

5

Weeks later Van pulls over to you on Seventh Avenue. His man is riding shotgun and leans back so you can rap with Van.

"I heard the shit they pulled on you. Them some low muthafukahs, Goat. I mean that shit."

"Yeah." What else can you say. No sense in getting mad anymore.

"Well, one thing, you know you the baddest nigger around, right?"

"Yeah."

Goat, I'm not shittin' you. You *know* you the baddest. Here"—he hands a bill to his man who sticks it out the window to you—"Take this and get your moms some groceries, man. Hey be good, okay? You playing in the Rucker? I know you are. Later." He pulls off, leaves you on the corner.

Walking up One Twenty-Fifth, you consider. You averaged 24 points per game for those suckers. You were All-New York City. You stopped games with some of your moves and shots. People talk about you today, talk about shit you did years ago, forgot about. And they wouldn't let you graduate. One piece of paper, one silly ass diploma that could make the difference in a whole lot of shit, and they fucked you. That goddamned Shanker had nothing but spite in his heart. Baddest player in the Apple and look what they did.

Foster, Parker, Lenox, Battlegrounds, Kennedy, Rucker— you'll play them all this summer. Some dudes already talking about going to college. Here it is only a few weeks after graduation and they talking about going to college already. Rudy going out to Ohio somewhere. How about that. He was cut from the squad when you both went out at Franklin, and you told him to come back out, not to give up but to try one more day. He made the team. Now he's going to college in the fall. That's hip—Rudy's your boy. Bob's going to school in Long Island. Everybody's cutting out. Jim Barlow at Kentucky State. You hear Barry's a shoe-in for Hofstra. Vaughan's thinking about Syracuse.

So you'll play your ass off during the summer, at least stay in shape and show them how good you still are. Who? Anybody. Anybody who cares.

You don't have to, say Rudy and Bob one day when you're shooting the bull in the park after running a quick three-on-three. Sit on the bench, drink some cold brew which burns your throat. Sit staring at nothing, enjoying the comfortable tiredness of your muscles as the buses, cabs, cars and bicycles pass by your eyes. Notice the gray deposits of salt on your wet skin. Elbows between your knees, head down but still looking ahead, can of beer sitting between your toes. Mellow Smokey comes from somewhere, singing over and over, *I said you really got a hold on me.*

They tell you to keep the faith, something will break. No need to take an attitude. They remind you of who you are, what you mean to basketball in the area. How the goddamned parks used to be full of crime and too dangerous to walk in. Now everybody plays ball. How at eighteen you're a legend in your own time. Shit makes you feel good, especially when you think back to some of the games. This is your place, these are your people. You can do no wrong as far as they're concerned.

Well that's okay too, but you will really turn out this summer despite what Rudy and Bob say. You look for the baddest dudes, play for two, three teams a day. Dudes like Helicopter, Lefty Peterson, Miles Aiken, Ron Jackson, Pablo, Willy Mangum.

One West-Indian dude named Aubrey comes up in some game. Audacious motherfucker is about six-six. "I want to play the Goat," he says. "I slap his shots away." Slight hush. People look momentarily, then you notice them licking their lips and smiling. You get rid of him quickly, taking him right to the hoop the first time you get the ball and slamming it in. He can't stop you, tries to push and shove you around. Don't call a foul. Keep using him. You take him to the hoop three more times as if you own him. You've developed this knack of smiling inside now.

"I am the Goat," you say, looking him in the eye. Quietly, no anger or spite, just telling him who you are, putting him in his place. What's wrong with that? Being nice about it, but after all, you *are* the Goat.

By mid-summer you are even nastier. You throw the ball in after taking one step from the foul line. *Umph* goes everybody. Walk a guy baseline, stop suddenly and fire: *rip*. Dunk the ball so quickly it almost isn't seen, you have risen in the air that suddenly. Over-the-head backwards dunks. Triple head fake, spin around and drive. Catapult toward the basket from anywhere on court. Turnout. Have everybody in Harlem talking about you. Block shots that seem as easy as lay-ups—appear from nowhere with a hand that slaps the ball. Glide, float, rise. "Goat stays in the air," you hear somebody say.

At breaks you, Bob, Rudy, Motorman and Dennis sit on the bench. Drink wine, smoke a joint. Maybe drink orange juice. Stare out into the game in progress or watch the mammas and size them up, make predictions on who has the best booty. They talk politics, women, sports—who did this and that when and where. You listen mostly, grunt now and then, agree with something.

One day Rudy talks about you being from the third world. He tells of the days you all walked to high school together in a pack of twelve to fifteen. He'd look around and you would have disappeared.

"Earl's from the twilight zone," he says. Funny thing is that you are the only one who smiles. The others shake their heads as if they know something is on the mark about Rudy's statement. Twilight. You aren't sure of the meaning although you watch the television show. Something a little eerie. You try to put your finger on it and it hops away like a flea. Not quite there. That may be so. Coming and going in two different worlds. Not really knowing how to express yourself yet realizing that people understand you. Sometimes feeling as if people can't help but come to you. As if you are everybody's little brother and whatever you do, right or wrong, they will try to understand. An attraction these people find in you may be what Rudy means by the twilight zone. The way they sit around you now is what you mean. They come to you. It's always been this way.

"You know the Goat can pack a gym," somebody begins, and you know you're all in for another round of stories. "Ain't that right, Goat?" says the speaker, now standing up and kicking the sole of your sneak.

"You better stop kicking me, nigger," you tell him.

"Yeah, soon as people hear he's playing, they start congregating. They be there before the game starts."

"I'm hip. Sometimes the night before and shit."

"Dig that." Laughter. The smoke is loosening everybody's tongue up.

"Some people be taking odds to see which spectacular shot he will try first," says Bob.

"Yeah, I saw a dude put a quarter on the court and swore the Goat would take his first shot—from there."

"I heard a dude say he had gotten his spot under the basket the night before because he knew the Goat was good for at least a half-dozen dunks."

"Goat, you know you got all kinds of little dudes twisting their ankles and shit trying to dunk the ball like you?"

"Hey, what about that game where Goat banked twenty-five shots off the backboard?"

'Twenty-five *straight* shots. Nobody knew there was a dead spot and all you had to do was hit it. Only the Goat, right Goat?"

You nod an answer. It's always embarassing listening to their stories. Still, you bear it. What could be hipper than being around those who admire you while they make up stories about you. Goat stories.

The summer goes like that. Play ball, rap, dunk, smoke. It's the same scene—women, crowds, fast runs. You perfect your favorite moves—over-the-head dunks, slam dunks from the foul line, swipes of opposing players' shots, stunning passes. Most of all you stay in the air, hovering, floating, gliding, turning in circles. Nobody you've seen yet can get as high and stay as long as you have been able to. Up there where the air is rare, they say. What is it, you wonder sometimes, that keeps you going like this.

You play in the high school division of the Rucker Tournament and turn out. All the dudes you played against in high school over the years are in the tournament. You can't be stopped. You play with a confidence, a knowledge that you can do anything you want. Sometimes your concentration breaks down and you are not spectacular, or you are a little tired, or you aren't sure how to go about doing what you should be doing. But you know you can do anything you want to do. Even you are amazed at it. Twilight zone—going and coming. What about the times you find yourself executing a move you had no idea of until you found your feet and arms and hands operating. Rudy calls it imagination. You remember others using terms like court sense and natural instinct. There is no feeling at all like this. Peace. A glow. You are in total control. Float, rise, settle back down, float. Nothing could be near the ecstasy, the soothing chilliness of the way you feel on the court. You are in control. People move for you whether they know it or not. You spin and turn and jump and glide without their being able to stop you. It is better than dreaming, better than sleeping, better than anything—this feeling. You live for it.

One day you have brought the crowd to further shouts and screams in a game your team takes by ten points. You have performed some acrobatics they have seen before but still don't quite believe and therefore, you figure out, get more satisfaction each time they see it. Sit on the bench while you cool off. Watch the elementary school kids take over the court. You smile to yourself as they shoot wild, over-the-shoulder hooks now as they warm up. Just like you did. They travel too, kicking the ball with their knees. You sit by yourself, your sneaks off your feet. Somebody is walking over to you. He looks familiar. A young dude. Button-down white shirt, pressed slacks, white sneaks. Thin. Nice-looking dude.

"Nice game, Earl." Quickly he turns and stops, and before you know it he is sitting down beside you, his back also against the fence. He puts out his hand. "I'm Holcomb Rucker."

Oh shit. You knew the dude looked familiar. You've seen him around. Mister Rucker himself. You didn't even know this is Rucker. You've seen him around and didn't know his name. He's a young dude and got a tournament named after him already. "Hey, I'm Earl Manigault." *This* is the dude everybody talks about? Scottie used to talk about him all the time. Supposed to be a legend. Got all kinds of dudes in college. Supposed to be a father and friend to a lot of dudes who were on their way or had been down the wrong path. "Yeah, I know who you are, Earl. I've seen you play many times. You played pretty well today. Where'd you get that double pump? That's some fake."

"Aw, I just picked it up." What is he up to? What could possibly be on his mind?

"What do you think you'll be doing in September?" Oh, maybe he has a job or something. "I don't know," you answer, feeling strangely comfortable with a man you've never spoken to before.

"I heard you got kicked out of school. That's too bad, Earl. I mean, you know how important education is for us black folks, don't you?"

"Yes sir. It was a bum rap, really."

"Well, that's what I understand, but that doesn't help the immediate situation. You need to get back in school."

You feel like a volleyball being batted back and forth. Something is on his mind. He has a plan, but why doesn't he just come right out and say what it is? From the corner of your right eye you see he is looking up at the housing projects.

"Earl, I can help you get in school," he says, and you are almost startled. "I have some contacts at a private preparatory school in the South. I can get you in. As a matter of fact, to be honest with you, I should say that I've gotten many young men in down there. Over fifty of them. Charlie Scott was enrolled. He asked me to see about getting you."

"Scottie's down there?"

"Yes. It's called Laurinburg Institute. It's in South Carolina. They have a powerful basketball team, feared by every black school in the South. Almost every man who starts gets a college scholarship. Would you like me to write a letter in your behalf, Earl?"

You knew you had good luck now and then, but you hadn't expected anything like this so soon. A few weeks ago you were crying about what they did to you in school, and now this man is standing here talking about he can get you in school where Scottie went. It's crazy the way things go. So soon you are walking through Colonial Park and he has his hand on your shoulder and everybody knows you both and says hello. And he is giving you pointers and talking as if he has all the patience in the world. You like this man, his voice, the way he looks you in the eye. When he makes a point, his voice rises for emphasis. You can't describe it to yourself so well, but there is something very soothing and comfortable about this moment and this man. It isn't that you have experienced this feeling before and recall it now. No, it's more like you haven't ever felt like this before and suddenly recognize that you haven't at the very minute you are experiencing it. Okay, you know what it is. This man is your father come back to you. He has just changed his name and everything and has a new family, but he is your father, you know now. The way he puts his hand on your shoulder. You want to close your eyes and drift, his voice putting you to sleep, his warmth dropping a glow of security and peacefulness around you. You are so restful ... father come back. Chills go through you. You are so restful ... so restful ... and then a voice stumbles against you, "Hey Mister Rucker." No, he is not your father.

Before you know it you are down almost fifteen blocks to Bradhurst. His car is parked there outside his apartment. Then you ride down to your hotel.

"Earl, you know you're going to have to work hard down there. Discipline. Study every night. You think if I can get you in, you'll he able to apply yourself? You'll have to, you know."

"Yes sir." Of course you will. You can't let him down. Plus, you'll get back at those jive muthafukahs at Ben Franklin. You will try hard. Nothing can stop you now. Wait 'til they hear. "Right here—you can park here." Shanker will shit bricks.

He sits looking down the street, down Ninety-Fifth Street, and you imagine he is staring at the Hudson just beyond Riverside Drive. The sun is setting. That's what he is looking at. You've seen it a thousand times, but you'll never tire of it. He accepts your suggestion to walk down to the drive and watch the sun setting beyond the Hudson River. As you close the car door and get closer to Riverside Drive and bask once again in the warmth and sympathy of this man, the bright orange band that hangs across the tops of the buildings over in New Jersey captures you. You both stand now on the walkway, his presence next to you still so obvious although you concentrate on the skyline. You've wanted to bring somebody other than Cindy down here for a long time to share this simple pleasure with you—the sun setting behind the Hudson. You don't say anything but, "Uhm, nice."

"Earl, I'll tell you a secret. Something I tell all the youngsters I work with. You determine yourself what kind of life you're going to live. Luck has its role of course, but if you decide you want to do something with your life and that nothing will stop you from doing it and that you *will* overcome every obstacle, you can't go wrong, son. I don't believe that hogwash about bad luck and can't get no breaks. Son, you got to *make* your breaks, do you understand me? We got no time to wait for luck".

"Yes sir, I know."

"Now you have one of the greatest basketball talents that I have ever seen, and I've seen them all, believe me. There is no way you can miss. You can become one of the all-time greats—if you *will* it. It's criminal to have a gift and not take advantage of it. Gifted people who are lazy should be locked up."

You look at his face to see how serious he is. He looks back and laughs.

"Shall we go see your mother now?"

Then, walk across the street and up the sidewalk. You throw some fake punches at kids who come up to you, swing on your arm, ask you for your sneaks, ask you where you played and who won. Lead Mister Rucker up the steps.

Moms is sitting in a chair outside the registration desk. She's just looking down the hall out the front door that you and Mister Rucker enter. She looks so peaceful with her apron down to her ankles, her brown eyes glassy.

"You decided to come home, huh? I'm working for Florine. Didn't show up. I wonder what the matter is, didn't show up last night either."

What can you do for your mother, Goat? Suddenly coming into this door and looking at her, you realize she is getting old. You love her. A moment's thought. Well, introduce her to Mister Rucker.

They get along. They have to. You leave them for a minute to go to your room. Change your clothes, stop, sit on the bed and look at the two photographs on your dresser. One on the left, from Carmen, seventh grade. Her face is shiny. She's wearing a band around her forehead and a blue cashmere sweater. In the space at the top right is her scribbling in red ink. "To Earl, with all my love—Carmen." On the other edge of the dresser is the school photo of Cindy. Her smile is brighter and larger than Carmen's, as if she is more open, less mysterious. Her handwriting is all over the picture. You read it without seeing the words because they are stuck in your memory: "Goat, I think you are one dynamite dude. Stay sweet, Love, C."

Get ready to go down the hall to the tub. Towel, soap, slippers. Your mother is telling Mister Rucker about how she used to wake you up to get you to school on time. Why is it you think about Carmen so much? Why keep her picture? When you saw her last she had heard about the kickout. She was sympathetic, looking good too as usual.

"Goat, I'm sorry," she had said. She looked as if she might be. Maybe a month ago on Thirty-Fifth, a Saturday.

'Yeah, thanks."

"I hope you'll finish your education," she said. You shook your head and concentrated on the game. Your eyes were getting moist.

"What are you up to?" you said, to keep the conversation off of you. She went on to talk about how she got a scholarship. She was going to Columbia. She had to live in the dormitory her first year. She was going to work so hard because she couldn't lose her scholarship. Did he know how much it cost to go there? "Naw," you said, then walked away. There was too much of a gap. You two had lost each other somewhere down the line and there was no getting away from that. You have this photo of her back there in your room because you know all your life she will stick in your memory. Now you consider that it will be better to get away from her. She's forgotten you. Now you can start forgetting her. And Cindy. She too will probably have to be a whole 'nother story. As your mother and Mister Rucker talk of your move South, you convince yourself that you will not hardly be able to come back here every weekend. She will forget you. You will forget her. That's the way it goes.

So now you have bathed, rubbed down with baby oil, dress. You feel a thousand percent better. Ah. Leave your room to see what's happening with home.

They are getting along like old friends. Rucker is leaning against the wall under one of the bare bulbs. She's still sitting, looking up at him and speaking slowly and quietly. They turn toward you the way people do when they are talking about somebody. Smiles. Shuffled feet, awkward hands.

"You done finally finished cleaning that sweaty body, huh?"

Mister Rucker laughs. Then he tells you that he'll send off the letter tomorrow and probably know in a week or so. That is fine with you. You walk him down the hall and to the entrance of the Pennington, then watch him unlock his car door across the street.

6

There's a roach crawling up the wall. Everytime you visit Cindy you see a roach crawling up the same wall straight ahead of you. Wonder if it's the same roach. Miss Robinson is sitting just to your left in her favorite chair and half faces the window. You ignore the roach to keep from embarrassing her. Her dream book is in her lap. She picks it up, glances through some pages and then stares out the window.

You wish Cindy would hurry. And why does she have to change her clothes just to go with you to the bus station? Stand up, watch out your knees don't bang against the little blue, glass coffee table, then take a few steps sideways toward the window. People are always moving up the sidewalk as if they are in a hurry. Never take their time.

At dinner you and Cindy talked about the trip down and how long it should take and who would be there to meet you. Across the street a clock in the barber shop window tells you there are almost two hours to go before your bus leaves. Miss Robinson smiled all the way through dinner. You almost forget she is deaf. Only when the two of you are alone like this do you feel funny. You know she has to read your lips and so you feel as if she is examining you the way she stares. Then too you always have to face her.

"Bus trip is *three-eighty-two* but bus is *one-nineteen.*" Her voice always sounds to you as if she's about to cough. Seems like it's about to break or something. "I think a *three will* lead tomorrow because we had a *one* today."

"Yeah, that sounds good," you say, then forget again that she can't see your lips, so turn toward her.

"You ought to put some money on it before you leave. Be a shame for your number to come out right after you leave."

You turn and smile at her, put your hands in your pockets.

"*Three eighty-two.* That sounds good. I'm gonna put five dollars on it." Wait for her to read your lips.

"You sure you want to lose all that money?" She likes for you to kid her. She smiles without looking at you and stares at her feet instead. "You might be able to spend it on some groceries or something."

"This number got to come out tomorrow. Even my workout say three eighty-two is due." Now she has a pencil in her hand.

Finally Cindy comes through the door from the dining room. She's trying to smile but you know she can't. She's walking fast too as she pats her mother on the head, walks behind her chair and comes over to you. "I'm ready," she says.

Now all you have to do is to say a few words to Cindy's mother and you'll be on your way downtown to get your bags from your moms. Kiss Miss Robinson, give her a big hug, promise you will work hard, thank her for the dinner, say yes, you will write her. At last you and Cindy are walking through the dining room with her mother scuffling behind you both and then you are into the dark hall, out the door, down the steps, to the street.

Hail a cab and don't say anything to Cindy. Get in quickly. Just look out the window while holding her hand. You're sure she's looking at you but you won't turn your head toward her. Broadway is as busy and crowded as ever but even as the driver speeds downtown you see a few heads on the street you recognize. This is how everything has gone in the last three or four weeks—as fast as this cab. A week after Mister Rucker visits your moms and you, he is calling to say that he's heard from Laurinburg Institute. They will accept you. Rucker got you a scholarship. You must report on some date in September, which means you can't play all summer in the tournament.

Your suit is part mohair but doesn't fit you as uncomfortably as you thought. This is the new Earl, in a suit. Tug on the necktie with your free hand, straighten it up. A glance toward Cindy. Her lips are poked out and she seems to be widening her eyes to hold back tears. She'll be all right once you've been down there for a month or so and write her a few letters. Put your hand in your right pants pocket where the twenty dollar bills—all nine of them—are folded. Two weeks of gambling—black jack, craps, poker—plus people giving you money to help you out. More than half of it was given to you. People would stop you on the street, ask if it was true what they heard, and then ask what you needed. A ten, twenty—always one bill—would then flash out of their outstretched hands toward your chest. You would say naw, it was all right, you'd make it, but they insisted until you were putting the money in your pocket, smiling, then thanking them and walking up the street. You got over a hundred dollars by gifts of tens and twenties like that.

Trying to act as if you aren't scared to death. As if you jump on the bus for hundreds of miles every day. You've already heard he don't take no shit down there. Rucker said you'd better be cool and not let them womens get to your head. They got curfews. Rules, Discipline. Get up early, go to bed early. This ain't Harlem. Cindy squeezes your hand just as you see some kids running from a fruit market, running smoothly and orderly, an orange in each hand. They won't stand for that down there—no hanky panky. You're ready. Squeeze her hand back. You'll show them you can do it.

The driver swings down to Amsterdam and you lean to the side in order to go in your other pants pocket for your spending change. Even Cindy, you remember as you wait for your change from the driver, wanted to give you ten dollars. Almost got into a fight about it, but she finally understood you *meant* no.

Wait for her to get out the taxi and then take her hand and walk. Drunks, kids, pregnant women, old ladies and old men. All the people from your neighborhood; they all fit into one of those groups; all look the same, all know you. Suddenly you are relieved at the thought of not seeing them again. A fresh break in you life—the South. Dirt roads and clean, clean air. Not all this noise and smoke. You usually think these people here standing along the sidewalk and doing nothing, only existing and acting no different from people you see all the day everyday in Harlem are special to you. You feel close to them. Your people. Now you don't know. You may be pretty damned glad to get away from this. You are glad.

"I'll wait here," she says when you reach the steps. She's pulling back on your arm. You can't drag her to the two marble steps. She's pulling away and looking across to the other sidewalk, her back to you.

"You ain't gon' say hello to my moms?"

"No, Earl." Her voice tells you she isn't kidding, either.

"Be ugly, then," you say, and walk through the entrance way. Two suitcases given to you by Mister Burns sit by the wall down at the end of the hall. Your mother comes from around the corner down there, stands in the middle of the hallway and smiles with her hands on her hips.

How much time? She looks at her watch. "You got about an hour. Better get started." She looks down at the suitcases. "I still don't believe old Mister Burns gave you those suitcases. He ain't making no money in that store no how."

You've never been away from your mother. Looking at her dark brown skin, complexion exactly as yours although you don't have the freckles or moles on your face—it comes to you that you've never lived anywhere without her being there with you. You are leaving her. You will be away from your mother; alone and without her. You'll be on your own. A burning fear slashes inside your chest. Momentarily you are stunned. You are almost tempted to ask her if she is going with you. It hasn't occurred to you until now—you are leaving her.

"What's the matter? Why you looking so pale? You ain't getting sick is you? What's the matter, you gettin' a fever?"

"Naw, I'm all right, just tired." Walk past her, your back to her, toward the suitcases. Pick them up. "I'm gonna go ahead and get down there, okay?" Now stand and face her. Bend forward with the suitcases in your hands and kiss her on the forehead, then head toward the doorway. She's walking behind you.

"Call person-to-person for yourself when you get there." You turn to see her eyes are glassy.

"Okay. You take care of yourself, right?" Touch her shoulder, watch her stand there, go out the door, then turn toward West End and begin your walk up the street; two suitcases banging against your knees. Greetings from the neighborhood as they lean against the various walls and throw out a wave or smile or grunt. From behind, you hear soft, slapping steps, like sneaks.

Two boys run up to you. You know the face of the one who grabs your wrist. "Hey, ain't you Earl Manigault?" You stop to look him in the eye.

"Yeah, that's me."

"See, George I told you that was him. He didn't believe me. Didn't you score sixty points against Wingate?"

You can't help from smiling. "Something like that," you answer. "What's your name?"

"See, George I told you this was the Goat. I'm Mark. His name is George. He didn't believe you was the Goat."

"I didn't say that." You watch the other boy staring at you.

"Well, what did you say? I said, 'there go the Goat' and you said, 'he too skinny to be the Goat.'"

"Aw, come on."

"Goat, you got a scholarship to prep school, huh? You goin' to college after that?"

"Yeah. Hey did you two guys see a lady come out my building down there?"

"She went up the street and got in a cab. She was crying," says George. "She went uptown."

Bitches are crazy, you think. Your lips tense into a half smile. You sigh and shake your head. What can you do about it now? Say goodbye and run up to the corner, hail a cab, throw in the bags, jump in yourself, direct the driver to Port Authority. You close your eyes and feel the warm, dirty summer air flow through the window and hit your face. Keep the driver from starting a conversation with you by closing your eyes.

Here it is early September. You will be eighteen in a few days. Somehow it seems as if your whole future, your whole life depends on this trip. All those years in high school for nothing. Some jive charges trumped up against you about marijuana. Carmen has gone into another world now and the two of you only speak to each other casually. Cindy must think it's over, that you will definitely forget about her once you get to school. What is it you should be concentrating on? Cindy said that your and her song would be "Our Day Will Come" by Ruby and the Romantics. Maybe this is your day, Goat. Maybe it all begins here. What was it that Rucker said, that you have to make things happen on your own, you have to *will* it to happen. No such thing as luck and breaks controlling everything. *You* control it—that's what you heard him say. Still it's hard for you to convince yourself you can do it. What is it you're doing, anyway?

Okay, here you are. Tip him although he won't help you with your bags. You know that. Drag the two brown suitcases off the seat, then stumble into a bunch of kids insisting they can assist you with your bags. Push through, trying to persuade them you can make it to the bus without their help. Once inside you don't know if you feel like an invader or part of the confusion. Metallic voices boom over your head as they announce departures to Phoenix, Chicago, Fort Lee, Philadelphia: arrivals from Newport, Atlanta, Atlantic City. Here's someone selling *Muhammad Speaks* and he is thrusting a paper toward you, his bald head and thin black tie looking like all the other black Muslims' heads and ties you see everyday in Harlem. An old lady in a long black robe has a cup in her hand. She wants donations. Your suitcase crashes into someone's thigh and you apologize. Almost everybody is selling something, or looking toward the ceiling for information, standing and scratching his head or rushing to buy a ticket as you are. So pushing your suitcases up a foot at a time, you stand in line and finally buy your ticket. Ten minutes to go to the bathroom and get to gate seventeen. Rush to the men's room. Buy some candy. Go down to the lower platform. The line is long for the Laurinburg bus. Walk to the end, trying to ignore the faces you feel are staring at you.

You take a seat in the back, throw your bags above, squeeze in toward the window. Fumes from the other buses. Close the window. Close your eyes. Push the tilt button. Float along ...

All of you are walking all bunched up together down One Sixteen. Loud voices arguing about some television show; mouths puffing out clouds in the cold air. Waving at the storekeepers. Trying to keep up with the gang—elbowing and stumbling. Won't do anything when you get to school anyway, but here all of you are really hoofing it to get there on time. Stop for a second to peek in a window. Mind goes off as you look in and before you know it the voices are way up the street.

Wake up to see a merry-go-round of tiny lights streaming past the window. You must be going into a curve. Where are you—New Jersey Turnpike, it seems. Hours to go. Turn your head back so your face is against the seat again, lick your lips, feel the heavy eyelids ...

They are coming at you. Three policemen are running down the alley toward you. Their guns flash under a lamplight. Suddenly you see one holding a leash to a—it's not a dog, it's a wolf whose lips are pulled up over its teeth. Now the three policemen are jumping through the air with the wolf. They are flying through the air at you. The wolf is flying ahead of them and is now about to pounce on you. You can feel his breath on your neck as you, still running, look back to see where they are. A wolf's claw is about to scratch your neck. The tip of the claw is on your neck, and easing into the flesh like a large straight pin might, sliding into your skin, piercing until you can feel blood oozing out of your neck ...

Now where? Eyes droopy, so droopy you can't open them, forehead against the chilly glass of the window, your mouth full of cotton, you turn to the empty seat next to you, then drop your chin on your chest to continue your dozing. Doze and wake up, look sleepily out the window at a landscape of trees and signboards and junk yards, doze again. Curl up and sleep some more when the bus gets to a rest stop. You are juggled and bounced around. You seem to be curling up constantly. Banged and jumbled around in your seat. Mouth sour and stuffed. Legs never getting as much stretching space as they need. Through the night and early morning you twist and rearrange yourself in the seat, glancing out the window during the repositioning.

And then you see you are riding up a little street. There is a catalog department store, a hardware store, a restaurant with a special on grits and eggs for breakfast and a post office. It's the Laurinburg Post Office. Somehow you knew you were here.

So, Goat, here you are. Seems as if you are always arriving at a special moment in your life by taxi or car or train or bus. Remember, as you look out to see baggage men at their jobs, what Mister Rucker said to you. Something about you must decide for yourself what you want to do. You make things happen the way you want them to happen. Is this the beginning? Okay, it must be. You blew all those years in high school and now must spend two or three years relearning that shit. All right, it was mostly your fault for not even showing up in class, but what about all those jive teachers who didn't even give a damn? They ought to share some of the blame, hell. Wait for everybody to get off, then swing your legs out, put on your suit jacket, straighten your tie, stand in the aisle with your head bent under the luggage bin.

Everybody is off the bus. Look out the window at the faces. Just ordinary people's faces, black and white, yet their looks remind you that this may be your last hope, Goat. You've got to make this work; you've got to be able to cope with this. Remember those days and nights on the court. Now this is what it adds up to, because you wouldn't be here without basketball and basketball is useless to you unless you can make good here.

Walk into the station, walk out into the early morning sun. It's just after nine. Look around, feeling funny standing there with two bags and not knowing where to go. Nobody here from the school, that's for sure. Or they don't recognize you.

"Uh, Laurinburg—Laurinburg Institute—can you tell me where it is, how I can get there?" you ask someone. You have to repeat it. Your voice is low the first time.

Follow his finger as he points, "Just down the street a ways, three blocks exactly." A church bell rings from that direction, reminding you that it is Sunday. Walk down the dirty road. It looks like Main Street in the movies you saw when you played hooky all those times. Wooden frame homes. The mutt barking at you from the grass but not hardly moving toward you. You see two wide, white pillars about a quarter-mile down the road. Concentrating on them, you find that there are a half-dozen one-story buildings beyond and around the pillars. Looks like a project development to you. Can it be the preparatory school you're supposed to be attending?

You are at the entrance before you know it. The two pillars. The entry road in front of you spreads away and is bordered by the few buildings. The sign: *Laurinburg Institute* announces itself in a rectangle of metal set in one of the pillars. Beyond the pillars, students move about busily, some staring at you with your two bags against your knees. Here's one who stops his march. You don't think you know him. He just stops and says that it's time for service, points at the building across the path. You assume the building he came out is the dormitory.

Girls come from the building on the other side of the boys' dorm. They mix with each other and move without nonsense from your left to your right. There are a few—no, several faces you know from New York. But they seem to be late and so hustle along with only a wave at you. This scattering and bustling in front of you, from left to right, continues until suddenly no one is left in the entrance to the school but you. The bell inside the chapel is ringing, the sun is barely over the trees farther down the road, the door to the chapel is shut and you now hear nothing. Just you. Alone, centered in the road, wondering.

The sun is already very hot. Go across to the boys' dormitory and sit in the little shade that building offers you. You hear the organ, then the voices of a choir. Sit there and wonder what the hell's going on. Nobody's around to welcome you. Nobody's around to do anything. Somebody must know you're coming.

Get up, leave your bags and walk around the campus. Few trees. Much of the grass is brown, stunted. All but two of the buildings are only two stories high. Hands in your pants pockets, you wander around looking at closed buildings and playing fields and wondering if you are really supposed to be here. It seems like forever by the time you finish your personal tour. Back, in front of the chapel again, watch the door open and the faces and legs and arms scatter down the steps.

Lonnie runs down the steps and grabs your hand. Oh, this is the dude who spoke to you earlier. You haven't seen him since last spring in New

York. Here are a couple of other dudes you know, gathering around you. Reese, Mango, Clarence Lake, Skip, Sonny, Lyle. Looks like half of New York goes to school here. A crowd is suddenly surrounding you all. The group from New York is asking you questions about this one and that one in Harlem. Way in the back is a sister with brown eyes. Her head darts to the side so you can only glimpse her. Now Lonnie is leading you around to the back of the chapel with the other dudes carrying your bags behind you. Feet crunch on the gravel walkway.

You all go up to two men standing by the back door. They stop their talking—in low tones as if the greatest secret you can imagine is being discussed. The shorter dude scurries off along the other path.

"Here he is Mister Downey," says Lonnie. He whispers to you out the side of his mouth that this is the president.

"Who is he?"

"Earl. Earl Manigault. Mister Rucker in New York wrote you about him. Didn't he?"

"Earl Manigault?"

He speaks weird, as if he's afraid to part his lips. Sounds as if his voice is generated by a music box in his stomach. Too squeaky for a man this large, you think. Light skin, heavy set, about six feet tall.

"Can you play ball, Manigault?"

Something sinks in your stomach. You weren't expecting to be received like this. You might not even get to stay. His head is right in front of the sun, so when you look at his face, you squint from the halo around his ears. "Yes, sir. Yes, sir I can play ball." Look him right in the eyes. You believe this. You know if you can do anything it's play ball, so why be modest about it. Tell people you can play. Tell them all.

He moves forward, out of the sun. Stares at you. "You wouldn't be joking with me, would you?"

Your man Lonnie jumps in. "He ain't kidding—"

"He isn't kidding."

"He isn't kidding, Mister Downey. He's the best player in New York."

"You told me *you* were the best in New York."

Lonnie punches you on the shoulder and laughs. Everybody in the crowd laughs also. Mister Downey keeps a straight face.

"Well, you better be able to play or we gon' ship you right back down to New York."

"Yes, sir."

"How Mister Rucker doing anyway? You see him before you left, Mani ... how you pronounce it?"

"Manigault. Yes, sir; he doing all right. He said to say hello."

"Okay now, everybody don't have to stand around here like there's nothing to do. Let's get on back to the dorms and hit those books. Lonnie, you show Manigault to his room."

"Which one, Mister Downey?"

He frowns. His skin is smooth and you guess he doesn't shave. "Where the heck is Bel? Where'd she say that extra room is?"

"He could room with me; I don't have a roommate."

"He can room with you. Listen, Manigault, you can be Lonnie's roommate. Now we don't have any foolishness down here, so whatever you used to in terms of New York just won't go here. This is serious business—education, uplifting. This is my school. My grandfather founded this school and I'm going to continue it. There ain't gon' be none of that nonsense you kids used to in that inferno New York, hear me?"

"Yes, sir, Mister Downey."

"Now you think you can deal with our way of life, Manigault?"

"Yes sir, Mister Downey."

"All right then."

7

"Get down, it's security!"

Fall to the ground and bang your knee against a stone. Bodies behind you thump to the dirt. Look up at the full moon, at the man's face smiling at you all. You are hunched over with your right knee aching now and sticking in the ground, your left knee up. For an instant you consider that you have fallen into the starting position you learned while running track in junior high school. You may have to run a nine-five if security doesn't keep going. Listen to your breathing as the sedan cruiser, so slowly it seems to be crawling. It stops for a few seconds and you're scared enough to pray. They send a beam of white streaming across the field to your right. It stops, remains fixed on something before flashing away and dissolving. The security car continues, rounding the track around the football field, past the uprights and then off to the main road, red tail lights melting smaller. Wave Lorenzo over to you. Half of his face is tan from the moonlight and you can see only one eye. He looks scared.

Everybody had been laughing and joking a few minutes ago, talking about who was gonna bang whom as the fifteen of you half-stumbled, half-crawled, half-ran across the field toward the girls' dormitory. You in the lead, wondering how in hell you always find yourself in these crazy situations. Fifteen dudes crawling toward the girls' dorm after midnight in the November cold.

"I hope Virginia ain't wearing no pajamas." Laughter again. They are trying to restore their courage.

"Gotdam it's cold out here."

"Don't worry, you gon' be warmed up pretty soon." Laughter again.

Somebody says, "Wonder if Wanda's roommate gon' be there too?"

Another voice: "You don't have to worry. I'll be with her."

Laughter.

"Hey, Calvin, get down, man, 'fore your big head blows everything."

Hold up your hand for them to stop. "All right guys, we gonna go in the door over there. It's supposed to be open. I'll go first and check. Then I'll wave the rest of you over here and y'all pile through. You on your own after that. Aye, get down, Scottie."

Run toward the door with your back hunched over and your legs bent at the knees. You limp; your knee hurts. You must look like a gorilla. The door is about half a football field away. Something furry and big as a rabbit scurries across the field in front of you. Scares the shit out of you. But you can't stop with them looking at you. Run into the door with both arms stretched out, palms out too. Turn the knob. It won't turn. Turn it the other way; okay. Squeaks open. A shadow stands at the top of the landing. She's in a robe. It's Yvette.

"Earl?"

"Yeah. It's me." She turns and goes through the door behind her. You turn also, open your door again, wave to the other guys. Moonlighted arms and legs reminding you of monster flicks, of spacemen on the moon, scurry toward you. Grins. Big eyes. Breaths coming fast. "Up those steps and through the door," you whisper, then stand with your back against the wall as they tip through the door past you and up the landing. When the last one is through the door, Yvette comes back out to the landing. You can see her thighs outlined inside her robe.

"You goin' back?" she asks.

"Yeah. I catch you tomorrow. It's too many of them ...too much of a risk."

Walk across the field in a half-trot. Your shadow moves to the right of you. Just your luck to get caught trying to get back to your dorm. Keep your eyes to the side; security has nothing to do but find your ass. Run as fast as you can the last twenty yards. Push the heavy metal door to the dorm open with your back so you can get one last look at the football field. Nobody has seen you.

You've been doing this alone ever since you met Yvette the second week. Those dudes are crazy, going over there like that; too many of them. Go by yourself, that's the way.

She was the one whose eyes you noticed on the first day. Short, dark-skinned Yvette. You told her it was a beautiful name. Up the stairs to your room; you still thinking about the day you two met. Bumped into each other on one of the walks on the way to class. You knocked her books all over the ground. She laughed, bent down. Her knee stuck out from the split in her dress as she went down, and you glimpsed a few inches of her thigh. You bent to help her. Lonnie didn't make up his bed—smart. When he returns he can just jump right into it. Take off your clothes. Keep the light off. Look out the window. Don't look as cold as it is. Everything is calm, safe. Lie down.

Do you like this place or not? Mostly you do, sometimes you wonder. Half the kids seem like they're from New York. Yvette is; that's hip.

But what a trip ol' Muffin is. Takes this shit seriously. Got the nerve to be the coach *and* the president. Coach? He only gave you one play, and that's for out-of-bounds. Half the time you don't know what he be saying, voice all soft and squeaky and shit. But it's the rules that crack you up. Sunday services in the chapel. That's a trip, especially if you laid up that Saturday night. Then he makes you cut off your hair. You started to check out right then. Gotdam, everybody in the Apple wearing razor cuts square backs, high tops. Style just came in. It's natural. But Yvette made you stay. She reminded you of Mister Rucker, your mother, your chances for the pros, the people in Harlem counting on you. How much of a sacrifice is it, she made you ask yourself. So now you looking like somebody scalped you. Pull the covers up to your neck as you turn over in the bed. J.H.F. Downey: what a trip. Funny dude, too. And his ole lady, Bel, just like him.

Everybody talks about their crib as the big house. Must have about ten rooms over there on the other side of the gym. Three cars, too. His mother has a crib right next to his. Breakfast at seven in the morning. Cafeteria way on the other side of the field. He got to be crazy or smart enough to know ain't nobody that hungry. But you still got to get up by eight because of inspection, even if you do miss breakfast.

He comes in with his suit and tie. New suit every day almost. You got to line up against the wall. Everybody is half dead from fooling around the night before. You think you're in the army or something. Hands must be at your side when he comes into your room. Soon's he goes to one room, somebody from another usually yells out, "Hey, Muffin, where you at?" Then Downey gets pissed or acts like he's pissed and goes out and slaps somebody upside the head. "Keep your mouth shut, young man," he says. He don't care who he slap. Giggles and comments follow. "All right, everybody quiet down." Meanwhile his old lady is running the same shit in the girls' dorm.

Beds have to be made up, no wrinkles in the spread. He may be pulling up a spread when somebody yells out, "Hey Muf ... fin; oh Muf ...

in." More students cracking up. He bends over to wipe his finger across the floor. This must be tiring. He does this everyday and finds the same damn dust. The fuck can you keep dust off the floor? Show me how please. No trash in the trash can. What? This is what you will never understand, No trash in the trash can. What is a trash can for? Somebody asked Muf that and got slapped.

Then he get into this fine thing. Everything's a fine. Twenty-five cents. Fifty cents. One dollar. Even twenty-five dollars for Calvin because he paint a wall without permission. Was painting the damn thing when Muffin caught him. Closet door open, thirty-five. Pants not on a hanger, fifty cents.

Crazy school, that's all you can say really. But all kinds of official dudes from New York and some from elsewhere who can play some serious ball are here or went here. Jimmy Walker. Dexter Westbrook. Scottie. Sam Jones. Our team is definitely one of the baddest in the South. But the craziest school. Bel, Muffin's wife, teaches history. Old Muffin himself got the nerve to teach math. His aunt on the staff, teaches French. Then her husband, Muffin's uncle, teaches history. Then Muffin's cousin is dean of girls.

What's this? Footsteps. Make no mistake, you know whose they are. He taps lightly on a door down the hall. You hear his steps click along the hall. Pull the cover up to your nose. Another knock and another no answer. Now he's at your door. Knock, knock. Just the two knocks, quiet, almost reluctant, as if he doesn't want you to hear him. You can't play like you're sleep, cause the door is unlocked for Lonnie. Turn over on your back, try to sound sleepy.

"Who ... who's it? Uh, who ... is it?"

"The president."

"Uh, just a minute, Mister Downey." Squinch your eyes up. Start to yawn. By the time you are pulling the door open, you are yawning and scratching at your pajama tops. Glance at the alarm clock before you turn the door knob: almost three. "Oh, hello Mister Downey. What's the matter ... what time is it?"

He brushes past you into the room. Looks at Lonnie's bed. Adjusts his tie. "Where's Mister Robertson, Manigault?" Turns in a circle. Maybe he expects Lonnie to appear from nowhere.

"Lonnie?—my roommate?"

"Where is he? Don't lie."

"I just got out of the bed, Mister Downey."

"I'm surprised you aren't involved in the shenanigans, Manigault."

"What's happening, sir?' Try to look concerned but still sleepy and shit.

"I just got a call from one of the dorm supervisors in the womens' living quarters. Men have been sneaking over there in droves, it seems."

"In the womens' dorm, sir?" Sit down on your bed. "You think Lonnie is involved?" Scratch your head. Frown. Suddenly voices. The loudest you've ever heard them. Laughter. Boasts. Cacklings. Haha's and hee-hee's. Backs are slapped. Some are singing. Footsteps are boisterous. Downey stiffens, comes to attention. You know what he's thinking. His father founded this school at the turn of the century to make gentlemen out of niggers. And look. They don't know how to behave. His lip is quivering. He marches out to the hall. Immediate silence. You don't hear a thing. Only Downey's breathing.

"Well, good morning, gentlemen," you hear him say, voice squeaky and falsely happy, you think. "Where have you gentlemen been? It's almost three in the morning. Mister Robertson, you know your roommate is worried about you. All right, nobody move. Just line up so I can jot your names down. There will be twenty-five dollar fines for everybody involved. Scoundrels, perverts. You'll pay."

You go back and get in the bed. You hear Downey taking notes. For once you have some luck. You knew there were too many of them and they were making entirely too much noise. Hysteria, that's what it was. No sense in getting caught up with all that confusion. Anyway, you started this shit. You were doing this shit last month. Ain't never been caught. When you tried to get them to come with you last month, they were too scared. You were the first one to sneak into the girls' dorm. History was made. It was a question of desire being stronger than fear. After the first time it was easy as pie. You put your forehead against the pillow to drown out Downey's voice, to think of more pleasant things than fines and maybe a few people being sent home if Downey really doesn't like them.

Anyway, about midnight one Wednesday last month you decided you would jump. Yvette had already told you at lunch in the sub what to do, where her room was, best way to get there. You got the rope from the closet. You went down the hall on tiptoes after Lonnie wished you good luck. Cold as hell when you got outside, and this was just last month. Ran like fifty. Across the football field, almost tripping. Fist balled up in one hand, tears easing down your face. Your other hand held the rope. The building, the door, the window loomed toward you in that order. Sneaked around to the back of the dorm. The gravel walkway crackled. All lights out. The third window, second floor. You threw up the rope against the window to signal her. She opened the window. You threw the rope up again and this time she closed the bottom down on the rope, secured it. You started climbing, too scared to think of how fast you'd be out of school if security caught you. She was on the top floor. Your knees scraped against the brick wall, your toes slipped, your elbows were scarred. Your fingers finally grasped the ledge and it was then you decided you'd never go that way again. She helped you through the window. She was wearing a T-shirt and no panties. Ruby was lying in her bed and pretending to be asleep. Yvette said, "Don't worry about my roommate, honey. She's asleep, aren't you, Ruby?"

Ruby snored.

Your heart raced. Since you had seen her the first day you wanted to press your cheek against hers, your fingers into her back. You couldn't say anything out loud; it was all in your mind. Her hands moved up the middle of your back. Tiny little thing. She pulled you toward her bed, you both stubbed your toes against Ruby's bed. You and she moved toward her bed. You were out of breath, you wanted to squeeze her and . . .

". . . And whose idea was this anyway? I'm looking at all you sexual maniacs and trying to decide which one of you is the sickest to come up with this idea. None of you is smart enough to write a coherent paragraph but you can organize a raid on some unsuspecting, innocent young ladies. Even Manigault is smart enough not to get involved in this mess. Madison, what do you have to say for yourself."

"Nothing, sir."

"What about you, Jones?"

You don't hear Jonesy say anything.

"All right you scoundrels, go to your rooms. And you'd better be up and accountable for inspection." Footsteps, doors opening and closing, some more garbled words from Downey, then Lonnie comes into the room.

"How'd you get out so quick?" he asks.

"Too many of y'all," you answer; "had to get my hat."

"Damn, twenty-five dollars." Lonnie throws his clothes onto the bed. "Bitch couldn't even fuck. Twenty-five damn dollars."

You feel sorry for him and want to laugh at the same time. Now you think about what a bitch it's going to be trying to get up in the morning. No sense in even going to sleep, but you'll drift off. Your eyelids get heavy but you can still hear Lonnie cursing and sighing and throwing his covers around.

Yvette ... Yvette. Mostly you talk about basketball and your playing. She thinks Chamberlain will outscore Jerry West this year. You asked her what about Oscar Robertson. This was in the canteen, where y'all did most of your talking. She sucked her teeth, said that Big O was too much of a playmaker while West was more mechanical. She reminds you of Carmen a little the way she always has an answer, always thinking. She helps you with your homework, too. Sometimes you feel like a dummy when she explains things so they seem so simple. But then again you always got to play around. Well, she takes part too. What about all those notes she used to pass to you in history? *What we gone do tonight?* or, *I want to see you Goat;* or, *You coming over tonight or what?* Right in front of the teacher, too. She's even sneaked in your room. That's probably one reason why Lonnie's so pissed off. All those times she came up and he acted like he was asleep or went out to the lounge for a couple of hours and she never got caught. Now he just tips over to the girls' dorm with a bunch of other fellows the *first time* and gets caught. Hey, that's the way it goes.

Yvette was surprised to find out we had only one play, especially since everybody knows we got one of the best teams in the whole South. How do we do it? Must be because of all the dudes from New York. Jimmy Richardson, Willie Mango, Charles Griffin; Lyle Williams, Clarence Lake; Walker, Barlow, Dexter. A monster team. Give us the ball, that's all. Just let us run. Smoked Winston-Salem's freshmens. Also put away A&T and North Carolina State. These are college freshmen we beating. High school is nothing. Booker T. Washington High supposed to be the baddest in the state. We had them by twenty points at half-time, then in come the subs. Dig that! The blue and gold of Laurinburg. Some tough dudes on this here team; better believe it.

They had a dude tough to guard on Winston-Salem's freshmen. The Pearl they called him. Itchy motherfucker. Always turning and twisting, never kept still, has all kinds of energy. He scored almost half the points of the team. A bitch to guard. Had one shot where he'd twist here, twist there, spin and fire the pill off balance, falling backward and shit. Passes scared the hell out of you. Two of them were dropped by his own men they were so damn fast.

So you stopped writing Cindy soon's you met Yvette. Don't have too much contact with anybody in New York hardly. Now and then a letter comes. Looks like Boys will be Franklin's biggest competition for the city championship. You sure are glad to get out of that jungle. This is a trip out here with those early morning breakfasts and inspections and Muffin's bullshit, but how would you have met Yvette? Yvette ...Yvette ...your eyelids are heavier ... Lonnie says something about twenty-five dollars...your head rolls on the pillow...you dread inspection in the morning ... heavier ... heavier ...

8

You are king now, you can feel it. Your last year at Laurinburg; two-and-a-half years in this place with its inspections and seven o'clock breakfasts and now everybody knows who you are. You hold the newspaper clippings in your hand.

LAURINBURG CRUSHES JOHNSON;
MANIGAULT STARS

Laurinburg Prep, spurred by Earl Manigault's 35 points, walloped Johnson High 87—62 last night for their twelfth victory in a row. Manigault, nicknamed the Goat, hit on an assortment of dunks and unbelievable straight-line jump shots and received a standing ovation when he left the game with 7:18 remaining in the fourth quarter.

LAURINBURG, LED BY MANIGAULT,
VANQUISHES LIONS 80–65

Earl Manigault scored 29 points to lead Laurinburg to an 80-65 victory over S.I. Johnson in a SCIL inter-league match last night.

Manigault, a 6-foot-1 inch senior, was 12 of 18 from the floor and threw in five slam-dunks.

Of the Johnson Cougars, only their center, 6-4 Bruce Cooper was able to score with any regularity. Strong under the boards, Cooper...

Sit back and look out of the window. Soon it will be Christmas and you'll be back in the city, home. Seems like you just arrived off the bus and started walking up the street looking for this little school. Now you got a half year to go. Any doubts you've had about your playing are gone, now. You've established yourself as the best high school player around, and one of the best in the country. Look at the kids going to the library or the canteen or the gym. You'll miss this place. It hits you that you'll miss it when you think about the letters from colleges. You can't stay here; you've got to go, got to move on to college.

In your desk is a stack of letters inviting you to visit Wake Forest, Michigan State, UCLA, Davidson, West Point, Johnson C. Smith, Morehouse; you keep a running count. There are exactly 52 letters in there now. Some schools said they'd give you a part-time job, an automobile, employment for your mother. Couple other fellows on the team going on to college too with scholarships, but none of them has as many offers as you. This little place hasn't been so bad after all, you think, looking out the window again. You might even miss it...miss the moments...

You see Larry moving for a fast break. You're already down court. What game...? You're not sure, probably Washington High, you've run this play so much in the last two years. To the right, by the foul line, you break for the basket. Larry is dribbling down the left side. Suddenly he stops, arches the ball high toward the basket. With two leaping steps you are there to reach for the ball and slam it in. Place goes wild.

Looking at the hunched backs of chilly students moving around the two-story buildings, you continue to daydream about your basketball years at Laurinburg. You wonder how good some of the current stars in college were when they were in high school. Walter Hazzard and Gail Goodrich at U.C.L.A. and Bill Bradley at Princeton. Can you make it in college?

Now you see yourself in the game against Tucker. Dude comes up to you during the warm-up. You taking it easy, standing under the basket and throwing up lay-ups, your blue-and-gold warmups on, and this tall motherfucker comes over to you. Stands right in front of you, gets in the way and shit of one of your players. Nobody pays him any mind. All kinds of tactics have been tried to upset your team. "What's your name?" he says. This must be a joke. Everybody in the state of North Carolina knows your name.

"Goat," you say, looking at him like he's crazy. You still throwing the ball up.

"No, I'm the Goat. That's my name. Paul Goat." You really think the dude is crazy unless this is one of their tactics. But then he goes on. "I'll show you who the Goat is in this game." Then he walks away, just like that. You tell the fellows what happened. They shrug their shoulders, say they never heard of him. Muffin of course has not scouted the team, can say absolutely zip about him. Break and go out for the tip-off. Home game, so the crowd is with you.

So you decide you'll teach little goat a lesson, show him who you are and who he isn't. First play goes to him at high post left. He swings around to hook it. You in the corner at forward. You sky in the air just as his wrist bends to release the ball and you grab it before it has gone two feet from his hands. From nowhere you have come to snatch the ball out of his hands. He must be at least six-four. The home crowd razzes him. Meanwhile you have shot the ball downcourt for Laurinburg's famous fast break and Clarence has layed it in. At the foul line you pull your famous leap from the lane after Lorenzo deliberately misses so you can jump, catch it in the air and bank it. Meanwhile little goat is standing on the line befuddled—that's the word Yvette used later. Y'all going up court by then.

Actually, he made you mad; that's why you turned out that night with 42 points. You played like you had something to prove. Over-the-head-dunks—must have done five of them while he guarded you. You blocked his shots as if he were a guard. He wouldn't look at you in the second half he was so intimidated. Once you stayed in the air and gave him two head fakes before you passed off for an easy lay-up while little goat fell all over you. You never smiled. Kept a blank expression. At the end of the game, he caught you glancing over your shoulder as you headed for the locker room and ran up to you. He was breathing hard and his eyes looked worn out.

"Hey, man." You stopped. "You're the goat, man." He shook your hand and walked back to his teammates.

Yvette almost didn't believe you when you told her about it. "Is this another one of your stories," she asked, poking you in your side and smiling, "huh?"

Smile and bring your gaze back to the room. You catch yourself smiling as Lonnie comes in. You half listen. He's gotten a ride to D.C. for both of you next week. You can catch the bus from there to New York and save a few bucks. Solid.

Lonnie's off again into one of his speeches about white folks. He's saying he can't understand them. They don't want us to go to their schools. They don't want us to go to their restaurants, live in their neighborhoods, go to their churches, ride in their trains. He's saying that he hates to go downtown because they stare at you. He's talking about the television news while you stare back out the window and think about the incredible Wilt

Chamberlain. He's leading everybody in scoring for the third year in a row. You think about the way he takes a pass at the side for the lane, waits for cutters, holds the ball over his head, bends down, fakes left toward the basket, then spins to his right and banks it in. He blocks *everybody's* shot: knocks it away, snatches it away. His dunk shot is terrible. You see defenders running the other way when Wilt's hand rises to the top of the auditorium. He's got the ball out there, higher than anything in the world for those looking up at this brown globe supported and controlled by his hand which suddenly releases it with more than two hundred pounds of power. The ball shoots through the basket, the rim trembles, bodies collide, Wilt regains his balance and the crowd is crazy.

Lonnie is still going on. He talks about the way they're treating Martin Luther King in Georgia. He saw it on television. Those little girls killed in church. He saw smoke and dust on the faces of the parents standing around the rubbish of the bombed church building. Policemen used whips and clubs and dogs on blacks who just wanted a sandwich. Lonnie's voice is starting to tremble now and you get a little uneasy because you don't know what to do about it. How can you, one damn black man, stop white people from killing you all? That's why it's frightening for you to hear Lonnie go on like this. You don't know what can be done. They got police and state troopers and National Guard and Army. What can you do?

You stare out the window again and think about Elgin Baylor this time. His extra step you never see because you're watching his head which fakes you right out every time. This is all you want to do anyway, Goat. Get your hands on the ball and perform magic. You can't do anything about what Lonnie's talking about. That's why you don't even watch the news except for the sports. All those people being beaten. It don't make sense. It do not make sense, Mister Goat.

Lonnie's going on about the classes now. How can they study history the way we get it. It can't be the truth. How can it be the truth if they are treating us like this? You turn toward him and ask him to please shut the fuck up. If he's so damn concerned, go join a picket line. Get your concerned ass killed.

The week goes by quickly and before you know it you have celebrated all the stuff you have to go through during the week before Christmas vacation. A play put on by the Dramatic Society; you sleep through it but wake up in time to applaud. "What was it about?" you ask Lonnie, not wanting to know. Then there's the choral society presentation of selected hymns—not too bad, make you think about some old ladies you know in Harlem. One big auditorium convocation where Muffin and his staff give speeches. You spend the time passing notes to Yvette. Everybody is whispering.

After the convocation, bodies are whizzing past you. Suitcases slam throughout the mens' dorm. Voices sing, make plans, tell jokes. Even Lonnie is laughing. Stumble down the steps with your bag. It's time to get out of here. Back to the Apple.

Then you are speeding toward home in a carload of loud, happy niggers. Some smoke, some wine; memories of games; everybody has a story about some broad or Muffin or one of the dorm supervisors. Every ten minutes a disc jockey is playing Marvin Gaye's "Can I Get a Witness?" and you all sing along. "My Guy" by Mary Wells is big too and you especially like the part where she lowers her voice and goes:

> *There ain't nothing you can do that can*
> *take me away from my guy.*

Get to Washington carrying one bag. The Capitol reminds you of the first train ride. Goodbyes to everybody who isn't going any farther. Climb on the bus to the Apple. Your seat is cold. Arrive in a great slush of dirty snow and outrun a half-dozen people for a cab. Uptown to your moms and then your boys who will be at various pool halls, gyms and recreation centers. After a couple of days though you get tired of New York. Is it something about the warm South that has slowed you down? Is it the cold, dirty New York snow? Maybe it's the cold treatment Yvette's folks give you this time. They want to know why you didn't come back with her, can't understand your ride (had room for only one person).

You mother's still at the hotel. You can see her aging. She still knows the averages of all the Yankee outfielders. A few lines in her forehead and in her neck. She repeats herself a few times. Mostly she sits in a chair outside the registration desk and smiles. It's the same seat she left to say goodbye to you when you started at Laurinburg. Some things you can't tell her—how you feel about all she's done for you; how she's responsible for you getting this far. Closest you came was to give her a large, tight hug when you walked in the lobby. Her eyes lighted up.

Bounce around the streets a little. Engage in community chatter about who's in school where and who will be back for the summer. Everybody talking about Chamberlain, Big O, Elgin, Laurinburg, Sam Jones, Power Memorial, Boys High, Alcindor. Motorman, who works downtown in Alexander's stockroom, insists the NCAA outlawed the dunk because Alcindor will dominate the game. "He can't be stopped," says Motorman. "Can't be. Look, Power ain't lost but four games in the last three years. You know what will happen when Lew gets to college. He'll dominate the whole game. They can't let him do that so they make the dunk illegal so he'll have to try other shots." People agree, nod, smile outside Jock's Restaurant. Y'all just ate pancakes and fried chicken. This day is not too cold so you all can stand on the sidewalk with your leather jackets and rap. "The nigger averaged fifty points, Goat!" he says, grabbing your arm for emphasis. "You know he's bad!" You agree. "He'll whip Chamberlain's ass, you watch." Arguments start all over again, center on Lew versus Chamberlain. You cut out to see Yvette.

The two weeks slip by and then you're on your way back to North Carolina. New York is New York. Action. Parties. Games in the Garden. Some good highs from smoke. But it tires you, runs you down. You want to get back to the trees, the chapel bells, Muffin's outrageous shit, the rules, discipline that you complain about all the time, but now see as necessary if you're ever to do anything sensible. You thought about it as you watched your mother in her everyday routine. Then she told you she was saving to buy a house in Charleston and retire in ten years. How could she think that far ahead. Little ass salary she's pulling and she's able to put some away. And can think that far ahead too? Wow! You are happy to get back to Laurinburg.

Two days after you're back there's an argument about "Under the Boardwalk," by the Drifters. Some say it's about the boardwalk in Coney Island; others say it's about Atlantic City. You laugh, don't really care as you sit in the dorm and listen to them. Look out the window as you always do when the dudes congregate here as they always do on Saturdays. The usual hunched backs and wool skirts making it across the campus. Your mind is off into next year. You don't want to be too far from your moms. You don't want to go to a large school. You don't want to be around too many whiteys. You lean toward Johnson C. Smith in Charlotte—small, black, in the South where it doesn't get too cold. Yvette thinks it's a good move. The coach is all right. Muffin says it's a good move. He may be crazy in his own way but he won't steer you wrong. All kinds of dudes from Laurinburg have gone on to college, mostly on basketball scholarships, so he must know what he's doing. About nine out of ten students come from New York, too.

Season goes successfully, Kitchell College is wasted. Three cats score over twenty points, you got 38. Best play was when you dunked the ball after taking off from the foul line. You breeze by all the high schools in January and February, when Muffin has scheduled the toughest games. Gibson falls by fifteen points; you hit seven shots in a row from the side. Maxon is no match for your fast break and that pass to the basket which you catch and drop in. Laurel Hill, Longwood Park, Roberdell, Eldorado, Jackson Spurs, Abbottsburg: none of them can stop you.

The bus trips home are always rowdy, full of singing, name-calling, jokes. Muffin always sits in the front and turns now and then to ark you all to behave like gentlemen. Quiet lasts a half minute. When you get back to the campus from these away games, Yvette with her fine self is always there waiting for you. One of you sneaks to the other's room after midnight, always manages to return before daybreak.

Then before you know it, it's spring. You and she roll on the grass of the football field at nights, talk about the silliest things, laugh at nothing, squeeze each other every chance you get. By March you have received 73 scholarship offers from colleges all over the country. The Laurinburg *Exchange* does a feature article on you with a photograph. You get twelve copies of the newspaper and send them back to New York. Gazing out the window one day you wonder if anything can go wrong. Everything looks good. An exciting, cold rush of feeling goes through you. Your fingers are tingly. You are the Goat. Earl Manigault. A very special person.

You are feeling this way one day in April at lunchtime. You have chosen to go to Johnson C. Smith. Finally you will be in college. Move across the walkway. Speak. Everybody says something, many want to stop and talk about nothing, you know, just want to be with the Goat for a few minutes. Okay, let them waste your time momentarily, won't do no harm. Here comes Yvette, wearing a lightweight skirt and one of those orlon sweaters— everything in bright colors like she can't wait for summer. You stand on the side of the walkway and wait for her to come up to you. She's not smiling. She isn't quite frowning but definitely ain't smiling. "What's happening," you say, putting your arm around her shoulder, half pushing her over. She's warm, but not as responsive as she is usually. Walk to the sub, say a little. Go through the line. The clatter is too loud. No sense in talking. Potatoes look lumpy.

Sitting opposite her you notice the tilt of her head. She's digging in her peas. You're going to talk about Johnson C. Smith and how you got another letter from a college in Utah that morning. You're smiling, talking like you rarely do, feeling good, then concentrate on her tilted head, the frowns in her forehead, her blinking eyes, the slow shoveling of her fork against her peas. She looks up, stares at you.

"I'm pregnant."

A rock falls from your throat to your stomach. She-it. Goddamn. Shit. Shit. Shit. How the fuck could you be pregnant? Aw hell. Damn. Don't you have no fucking sense at all? Why you want to do this? You are dizzy, failing. Lights are turning yellow-red like the sunset over the Hudson River. Your ears buzz. Metal trays with lunches on them bang and clatter. Voices around you rise together like the choral concert at Christmas.

"You're bullshitting."

"I'm serious, Earl."

"Naw, you're joking." Start smiling. Then start laughing.

"Hey Earl, I hear you going to Johnson C. Smith, brother." Dude you haven't seen in weeks stands by your side. Nod yes, stare at Yvette as if you don't want to be disturbed. He goes away.

Get up and walk toward the door. Are you walking? Everything is yellow and red. She's pregnant. You know she isn't kidding. You left her alone at the table. She's pregnant. God damn. Try to reach the door. Everything was so fucking perfect just an hour ago. She's pregnant. Goat, why does this shit constantly happen to you? Damn broad can't take care of herself. Pregnant. You on your way to college—or was; opportunities finally break, then she comes up with this shit. Pregnant. What happened to everything that was going all right a minute ago? Out the door. People yell at you; huddles of people are clustered together and you have to move through them to get the fuck out of here. You don't know where you're going; you know where you're not probably. Muffin will hear. Then the shit will be up. He'll put your ass—both your asses out of school so fast it won't be funny. No college now, buddy. You don't even know where you're going; only walking fast with your head down and a glare of people moving around you. You look up to find you have walked to the gates, the entrance.

You have left Yvette. She's pregnant and you left her in the canteen. She's sitting there pushing peas with her fork, about to cry. You just left her. Thinking about how you didn't expect a child, how your basketball career is just about up, how you'll be kicked out of school, how some baby, some

Goddamn unexpected baby, is on its way. But standing at the gates, looking down to the town, you realize you have left her. Her twitching eyebrows, the wrinkles in her forehead. Turn and run back to the canteen. She's gone. Ask the dude who was sitting next to her. He didn't see her leave. Turn in a circle, your heart drumming against your chest, to see her head, bent, a few books cradled above her waist, turning through an entrance. You run calling after her. She stops in the hallway. Now her eyes are wide with surprise. She smiles.

"Hey, come here, girl," you say, and grab her. The books fall on your feet. "We gotta work this shit out, right?" Her forehead tilts against your chest. Her arms go around your waist. You stand there holding her, rocking side to side, trying to think of something. Take her outside. Go behind a building and hold her again. The discussion starts with, "What do you want to do?" Within an hour you two think you have some idea of where you're headed, how you will handle this unexpected dilemma. You come from behind the building feeling much better, closer to being able to smile. The chapel bell rings. You walk to class with her. It's almost over if you can make it through five more weeks.

They go slowly. You can't sleep anymore. You spend so many nights looking out the window. Sometimes you cry. You are sitting in your chair by your desk, looking out the window, thinking about all this shit on your shoulders and suddenly tears are coming. Then you can't stop them. You leave the room and go to the john to keep Lonnie from catching you. You come back and look again at the buildings, tall, white cement boxes, the few street lamps hovering over the walkways, the security car cruising the same route it takes every night. Your chin is in your hands. You bite your lip and blink your eyes and try to think of something funny—all to keep from crying again.

So far everything is kept cool. If Downey knows, he sure isn't saying anything. Nobody is saying anything. You have talked to Lonnie about it but of course he wouldn't mention it to anybody. You want to take care of this child. You want to marry Yvette and take care of her also. She isn't sure what she wants to do. You've discussed it over and over and never really decide on anything definite. So this is what is known as punishment. You're the first to sneak into the girls' dorm and you're the first to knock up a student at Laurinburg Institute. There should be a plaque for that. Now if you can just graduate from this motherfucker. If they don't let you graduate you'll lose your mind, do something crazy. They must.

One day in the rain you see Muffin. He calls you over to share an umbrella. He's standing under a tree and watching students walk by. You join him. This is it, you know. He never talks to you.

"Where are you going, Mister Manigault?"

"To the library," you lie.

"Very good." He looks straight ahead at the flow of students. "Very good." Then he turns and smiles at you. "Well, don't let me stop you."

So nobody says anything and you manage to finish the year. You can't believe you have actually escaped even when you walk up to the platform to get your diploma. Downey even smiles when he hands it to you. Yvette goes up with her big stomach and you wait for everybody to crack up but nobody does. You must really be the Goat.

Nothing can stop you now. You think of the shit you've gone through and still held up and now all you got to do is get back to the Apple, face Yvette's parents, tune up during the summer and get your ass in school in September. You are daydreaming as you tip down from the stage. What you didn't learn and what assignments you didn't do because Yvette handed them in for you doesn't matter now. You've got your diploma. Goat, you're on your way again. You can start thinking up names for the baby.

Goodbyes come harder than you thought they would. Some of these dudes were like brothers to you. Many of them going on to college: Kentucky State, Morehouse, Norfolk State, St. Johns; others will go back to New York and at least be able to say they stayed out of trouble for a couple of years.

When the four of you sit down—her parents, Yvette and you—in New York, Yvette takes care of everything by saying, "I want to go to school. Earl wants to go to school. I'll stay and take care of the baby."

No immediate response. They nod and look at each other. You think about it. It makes sense yet you know she's giving up a lot, sacrificing on the hope that you will go to school, make it as a player, enter the pros. They come around to agreeing. Yvette will stay with them, you will stay with your moms for the summer and then cut to Johnson C. Smith in the fall. Nothing can go wrong.

9

"Nigger, get out my face for I hafta put lacerations on your cheek."

"Who you talkin' to?"

"You ugmo; you answered didn't you?"

"Watch the dunk...."

"... Hey, who can reach the top of the backboard?"

"...We wasted those muthafukahs..."

"Earl, you were mean, brother ... you see the way he dunked the ball *over his head backward? ...*"

Your mouth is dry as cornbread but you shout and jump and run around, acting crazy like the rest of them. Your team has just won the Lincoln tournament, beating the Stars by seven points. You turned out as usual, scored in the forties, blocked googobs of shots. Now everyone is a wild man in Colonial Park. Skip. Sonny. Larry. Willie. Rudy. Dennis. Boo.

Larry runs up to the backboard. "Umph," he goes, trying to hit the top of it.

"Hey, watch out, I got it," says Skip, taking a start from the foul line. His fingertips touch the rim.

"Hey, chip in you guys for some pluck."

"What ... ?"

"How about some Meideros; we need three bills for a gallon," says Dennis. Hands shuffle in pockets.

"Just make sure it's cold," you say. The others grunt approval. Dennis skips out of the park. You all sit down on the bench. Sonny asks about Yvette. "She's okay."

"What'd you name the baby, man?"

"Darrin."

"Darrin? ... hey, that's beautiful man, that's nice. Oh, you know," continues Rudy, "I saw Cindy the other day. She asked about you." You grunt.

"Goat's old flame, huh? ... that the one with the big-assed tits?"

"They got bigger, too."

"Yo Goat, what about all that shit at the Garden?" asks Boo. "All because of a riot in the stands, they cut out the high school championships."

"Yeah," says Larry, "that was to keep niggers from having a chance to play in the Garden and show what they can do. Whitey's always pulling slick shit like that."

"You mean half-slick shit."

"That was a year ago, wasn't it?" It's Skip speaking. "In March? Damn, Rucker died in March of this year. March must be a bitch."

"It's the Ides of March," says Rudy. "You remember that shit from Shakespeare, right Goat?" Everybody, including you, laughs.

By now Dennis is back with the jug. People walk by, wave. You look down the bench at your boys. They're all sweating still. High knee sweats. Cut-off jeans. Orange shirts with blue numbers, the top of the shirt around the chest dark with sweat. It's early afternoon and still warm. You are so glad to be back in the Apple; the city's motion, activity; your friends; the sounds and smells. Eyes begin to blaze and you open up, start to talk more.

"Hey, you know I almost went out to U.C.L.A., where Lew is going. But it's too far; I'd be away from my moms too much," you add.

"That's gonna be hellified when him and Wilt hook up," says Willie. I see Wilt's making over a hundred grand a year for three years. Ain't no athlete ever made that much. Goat, what would you do with that kind of money?"

"Buy me an MG and a house in the country," you answer.

"You wouldn't buy a Rolls Royce?"

"Naw, I'd get an MG, something small." Your head is bouncing on your neck. The cars on Edgecombe are running into each other. You get up and run over to the basket and dunk the ball. The basket is much lower than you had thought. You stand looking at nothing, thinking in an instant of too many things— memories of your brothers in the South, the baby, some money. Your boys, your friends, people you can always lean on are on the bench. Throw up another shot.

This dude appears from nowhere, suddenly standing under the basket with his hands in his pockets.

"You're just under six feet, aren't you?" His question stops you from dribbling.

"Yes," using that word instead of *yeah* because he seems like an older adult; "six-one."

"You leap pretty damn high for your size." He stands, looks at you. You look at him. What's he up to? "You think you can reach the top of the backboard?" Who is this, the devil? A mad man? Why would he out of the clear blue sky ask that? You hear the breaths of your boys now behind you.

"I don't know, you know. I might." Hey, see what the nigger is up to. You never can tell. Eyes are glassy. Probably been drinking.

"Listen, if you can reach within twelve inches of the top of the backboard, I'll give you all the money in my pocket." Um's and umphs from behind you. Somebody says that you can't lose, Goat. What is there to lose? Call a kid from the sidewalk. Get him to climb up the pole and put a paper cup in the top hole on the metal perforated backboard. You figure the top hole is about six inches below the top of the backboard.

Step quickly out of the circle formed now by the fellows and a little crowd of people up from the sidewalk to see what's going on. Take a swig from the gallon first. Your head still light, you smiling, you feeling as good inside as you need to feel, you turn with your hands down to your hips and take two steps almost before you yourself know what you're doing, jump up and grab the cup.

"All right." Fellows cut up: smack you on your shoulder; punch you in the chest; hold back the wine bottle as if they're going to douse you with wine. "Goat, you did it."

Shake away from them and go over to your man. He's smiling with his head down, counting out one's and five's and ten's. "It's forty-five dollars," he says, handing it to you. "Congratulations."

"Oh, shit, the nigger almost got to the top," says Larry. "Goat, I didn't even know you had it in you. Why you never tried that before?"

You ignore that question. "Hey, treat's on me. I buy everybody a beer." Head for the bar around the corner. Go through the little crowd that has gathered, accept their congratulations and slaps on the back ("That's Goat, ain't it ... That's Goat ...") cross the street to Tillie's. Squint your eyes to accustom them to the dark bar. Willie and Sonny reach for the pool sticks, take over the table in the middle of the floor, you and the other guys sit in a booth. Jackson starts bringing the brews over, wiping his hands on his apron, smiling as everybody at once tries to tell him how you almost reached the top.

Sit and jive around for over an hour until it is after four o'clock.

Somebody says that Twenty-Ninth Street might be doing something later on in the day. "Let's go over there now," you say, high now, unsteady on your feet and knowing nobody will dare say no although West One-Hundred Twenty-Ninth Street is about as rough as you can get in Harlem.

Okay, everybody slides out into the bright July sun. It's blinding. Car horns, profanities litter One-Hundred Forty-Fifth. You think you glimpse Van turning the corner up the street in his new hog. Skip breaks out into some funny burlesque-like dance steps as soon as "Papa's Got a Brand New Bag" by James Brown comes screaming from an open apartment window. Skip grunts like J.B. himself. "Hey, when that nigger coming to the Apollo again? I want to see him," he says, now dancing with a street sign, his partner, as you all, tipping and swaying after drinking a gallon of wine and who knows how many mugs of brew, navigate your way down the sidewalk.

Go over to Seventh Avenue which leads to the St. Nicholas Project and spend the rest of the afternoon playing ball, drinking wine, messing around with the women, joking and laughing, just grooving in the park. You stay there and spend another six or seven dollars on more booze, some subs with hot peppers, and potato chips. Rhett, Bob, Will, join some of the games. Soon the sun is going down over the park and it is nearing dawn. Bodies move out to go home for lunch or help their parents perform various chores. You run another game, a short one of eleven just to keep from cooling off. Various conversations going on at different benches. Voices get louder as topics get hotter ("Don't tell me, nigger, I *know* what I'm talking about!") You are aware of everything although you concentrate on the game.

Then you are running another game and it is dark except for the light shining from the street lamps. Even the moon seems to give off more light than the lamps. Your high has worn off and you are tired but not beat when a dude in striped pants and sheer shirt and a big leather hat comes up to you on the bench.

"How many can you make in a row?" You know him as a pretended sportsman. He bets on anything as if he's going to make a million dollars one day, you heard. Must be your day for challenges.

"That's the Goat you talking to," says Rhett.

"Can you throw in five jumpers in a row, Goat? A nickel says you can't."

You give Bob a five-dollar bill; so does the gambler. Crowd gathers; they've heard everything and you're positive all activity in the park has now stopped. You shoot a jumper from the top of the circle without dribbling and hardly looking up. It goes on a line into the basket. A dozen or so people are lined up along the sideline.

"Take time, Goat. It's easy for you."

You dribble, lift the ball with your left hand, tilt it back, looking over it at the rim ahead, pop your wrist. It swishes.

"That's two,' somebody says. Tires squealing on the avenue. More advice: "Take time, Goat."

Move to the left a little. This time turn in a circle and aim for the backboard as you spin, facing the basket, arching the ball more than you usually do so it glides upward over the basket, slams against the backboard and falls through the strings.

"Just two more, Goat. Take time, baby, take time."

"You've done this thousands of times. Five times in a row. But never for money, with a group watching you, with someone challenging you. Dribble the ball as you stand to the left of the foul circle. Best thing is to take your time, concentrate, ignore everything around you but what you must do. Nothing so difficult about putting a ball in the hoop. Twice more, that's all. Okay. Dribble to your right behind your back, spin again, then fire. It doesn't feel right, not enough spin, a little too high. But it hits the front of the rim, bounces to the top of the backboard and falls through. "All right ... all right ... all right. Luck counts too, Goat, don't let it worry you. One more Goat."

Don't let the last shot get to you. Best thing is to go ahead and fire, so as soon as the ball is thrown to you, you fake left, move to the right while dribbling the ball from your left to right hand, go up and fire especially hard. This time the ball line drives right into the basket, hardy an inch above the rim. Two kids from the sidelines run over and grab on your arms and congratulate you. Rhett and Will and Rudy slap five with you. The dude comes over with Bob and shakes his head, agreeing that you have won.

"What else can you do? You gon' give me a chance to get my money back, ain't you?" He's smiling still, his eyes darting under his big leather hat, standing with his chest out and the palms of his hands open with fingers pointed stretched toward you.

You put the ten dollars in your pocket, then take two leaping strides toward the basket and dunk it, shaking the rim and backboard. Come back to the group of your boys and the gambler. The half-court game on the other side of the court has stopped. You see a light-weight crowd circling you. Hold the ball in your hands and turn it around.

"I got twenty says you can't dunk fifteen in a row." You can feel the niggers' excitement as they grunt and groan and their feet stir around.

Go in your pocket and count your money. "I'll do it thirty times back-to-back for my last thirty dollars," you offer and hold out the cash, two tens and two fives.

"Bet," he says; gives Rhett the money to hold.

Immediately you turn to dribble down court in the night in the park. As you near the foul line you start to ascend, palming the ball upward as if you are lifting it, then pressing the ball into your left palm as your legs are off the ground. Bring the ball above your chest and over your head. Your eyes have been cemented on the rim. Now you slam the ball through the hoop. It slices through and rubs against the strings, swishing them so they sway after the ball has fallen through and you have caught it and begun to dribble all the way upcourt.

What is there about the dunkshot that puts basketball on a different level? Why is the shot so special? Rising is one thing. Getting off the ground higher than anybody expects you to at six feet, one inch; leaving the sidewalk with its chalk marks and painted signs (*Robert loves Gina; Boys High full of punks; pussy is good*) and tiny pieces of glass from soda and beer bottles. Off that cement that even has blood stains and piss spots; the same cement or gravel or whatever kind of sidewalk they call it technically, the cement you have skinned your knees on as a child; off of it and away from it and into the air. Rising, flying, taking off above all of this, moving away from it at least temporarily.

Then the surprise of it all. Who expects you? Nobody. Almost as if you walked on the moon. Little dude suddenly catapulting into the sky like that, above everybody, and so damn suddenly, that's what freaks them. The sudden, unaccountable ascent. The short time it takes you to leave the ground surprises you sometimes in its swiftness.

Slamming it down. It is a climax, a release, a statement somehow of yourself. Your self. I am the Goat. Move, please, I am in flight. This is me, SLAM. If there are no strings as there usually aren't in Harlem, you have to hit the rim some way. Either your wrists or your arms or your fingers after the ball has been thrown through must touch the rim and then the rim has to shake or make *some* noise. It's the abrupt end of everything: the play, the dribble, the fake, the leap. Once that ball is jammed, there is no more, the book is closed.

And the sweet sound. The strings like sucking. Closing of a whirlpool.

Swirling guzzling whoosh. Swooping pigeons napping their wings just once. Dunk sound. Jammer. Jammer. Slammer. Then your hands banging against the backboard, booming and slapping against the metal frame. Do it hard enough and the pole will shake, wobble. Or hang on the rim for a second, then fall to the ground. Come at the basket from the side. Storm down the middle, through the lane. Dunk shot. One after the other, back and forth. Slam, ramble, swoosh, ooh. You are hypnotized by the soar through the air, the throwing down, the feel of release, power. They—nobody—can stop you. This is you above the world. And then you have done it fifteen times, twenty, twenty-five, thirty.

People clap. The same two kids run up to you. But you break away from them and their Popsicles and just for measure run up and down five more times and dunk it backwards, each time taking a different angle on the basket.

As you collect the money and the congratulations, your knees feel as if they will sink away. Your body is soaked, your shirt is now a wet towel. Get the money and sit on a bench. You can't talk, your breathing is coming so hard. You can only speak one word every five or six seconds and even then your head is hung and you stare at your sneaks.

"Let's go over to Seventh and get some fish and chips," you say.

"Hey, it's almost eight-thirty, Goat; I think I'll be getting along, you know?" Others hum along with the same stories about their having to get home or get here. Soon it is only you, Rhett, Bob and Will who trek to the fish and chips restaurant. On your way you see the familiar Caddy of Van. This time there are three fine women inside with him. The cooled air startles you when he rolls down the window. You look inside, smile at the women, engage in light chit chat with him. He gives you' a twenty-dollar bill. Now the world is yours. Your pockets are full.

Back in the park you gobble down the fish, French fries, cole slaw, orange soda, rolls. Rhett and the others cut out after thanking you for the grit, claim they have to get showers and get ready for the weekend.

You are waiting for Spider. Just before the Lincoln game ended he had said he wanted to take you to Veralda's party up on the Drive. Sit on the bench by yourself now and just stare at the street. Your feet ache. Wiggle your toes. Close your eyes, then open them again before you fall asleep. Car horns; police sirens, screaming brakes; night comes to the city. A teenager walks by with his arm around his girl. You feel differently now about all of this because you are a father. Darrin is almost a month old. You have to do something that makes sense now. His future is at stake. You look at the whole world differently. Never will things be the same. Even this couple walking down the sidewalk have to be understood differently.

Two figures come up the street about a block away. You know Spider's bop, shoulders twisting right and left as if he's a fullback. Rapping his ass off too; hands fanning the air in front of his stomach, head turned toward his man: looks like Vaughan, tall and taking those long strides while looking straight ahead. As they get to the entrance to the gate, you wave.

"Goat, what it is? You 'member Vaughan don't you? Heard you turned out the Lincoln Tournament today, brother. Still bad as ever, huh?"

You nod, grunt, shake your head.

Vaughan has a wide white cap and tiny dark glasses. "You ready to party, man?" He's smiling as if he has a secret.

"I ain't spent no time with Goat since last summer, ain't that right, Goat?"

"Yeah. Rhett and Bob and Will just left, you know."

Vaughan snaps his fingers. "Goat, answer me this. Didn't Gillespie...you know, Dizzy Gillespie, go to Laurinburg? I know about Jimmy Walker and Sam Jones and Scottie, but didn't . . ."

"Yeah, he went there. Think he played in the band."

"Bet. I thought so all the time. Didn't I tell you, Spider?"

"Right," he says, sitting next to you. Vaughan sits next to Spider. He pulls up his pants legs, slides a hand into his socks, brings a small plastic bag out, looks around. An old lady goes by pushing a laundry cart. "You wanna sniff a little, Goat? Then we cut out to the party, okay?"

You agree, shake your head. In a minute you are holding up the envelope to your nose, sniffing hard through one nostril at a time. Pass it back to Spider. The conversation goes to how long he and you have known each other. He tells you he has seen Cindy. She lives with a dude in the village. Carmen's in her last year at Columbia. So-and-so got shot outside Small's. What's- his-name is in the hospital; they think it's cancer.

"Yo, Goat, you ain't high yet. Relax, my man, you with your boy. You can relax." Spider hands the bag of white powder to you again.

"Hey, what is this shit, Spider?"

"Heroin."

The strangest feeling comes over you, as if someone from the dead is calling you. Shivers. "Heroin? Ain't this shit dangerous?"

"Hey, Goat, would I do you wrong, brother? I been doing the shit since

I known you." He slaps five with Vaughan. "Take three draws in each nostril next time. Loosen up, brother. Hey Vaughan, ain't that a beautiful moon up there?"

You hadn't even noticed the moon. The motherfucker's up there laughing at you. Look at him. Crazy muthafuckah. You wonder if in fact the moon is made of cheese. Oh, shit, that would be crazy, running around and then stopping to fall on your knees to eat some cheese. But not quite as funny as this dude Vaughan's brim. Where in the hell did he get the idea that he could look good with something like that? God damn that shit looks funny. Look like he wearing a flying saucer or something. You start giggling. God, don't let the nigger ask you what's funny. Oh, he's laughing too. Wonder if he's laughing at himself?

Suddenly a truck runs through your stomach. That's what it feels like. It comes up to your throat. You put your hands to your neck. You're gagging, then fall to your knees, coughing once, then spitting vomit onto your sneaks. Your insides are jerking. You gasp again. Your head is so heavy you can't lift it. Spider pulls you by the shoulder until you're back on the bench. Again your chin drops to your chest. You hear muffled voices say something about getting you to the pad. They lift you by the shoulders and you can tell they are stumbling too. You say that you are all right but you know you ain't.

It's all blank as your feet move you through the street. You get to Spider's crib on Broadway and they throw cold water on your face. You jump into the shower and soon feel good as new. Spider gets you some pants and shoes of his brother's and they fit you.

Your nostrils still burn. Sitting on his couch, the limpness in your arms and legs reappears. You want to nod again. Their legs move around, the television newsman reports on rioting in some town in the South. The bath has relaxed you but you still feel as if you can't move.

"Ready to cut out, champ?" It's Vaughan, the little dark glasses reflecting the glare of the ceiling light. "Hey, once you start walking you'll be all right. That shit kicks your ass, don't it? ... you like it ...?"

You nod your head and lift yourself up. Spider comes out of the bathroom. He's bobbing and weaving around the furniture, ready to bop. "Goat, Veralda lives right off Thirtieth on the Drive, you know. I ain't partied with you in so long, that's how come I wanted us to get together. You understand what I'm saying? Solid."

If you could just tell them how glad you are to get into the fresh air again. Your first steps are wobbly but you soon straighten up. Hell, it's only a few blocks to Riverside Drive. You can skate now. You feel good, too. Played ball all day, got high, took a shower. You should have checked on Yvette. Call her tomorrow.

It's one of those big buildings with the wide glass doors. The lobby is carpeted, you can see. When the intercom buzzer goes off, Spider says, "It's the Spiderman and two of his main men. Come on, let us in, girl." Up the elevator, down the hall, ring another bell and your face is blown off almost as the door opens and

Stop! in the name of love

blasts through to you. Intros are quick as you go in. Immediately you see the big window facing the Hudson and the lights of New Jersey. People are saying hello as you look out the window. Move around, shake hands, snap your fingers to the Supremes. You size up the scene quickly: casual, hip dress; some fine women; table of wines against the wall; sandwiches, cheese and chips on the other table. Spider talks to Veralda. Vaughan has disappeared already. All the furniture has been moved to the side and people are getting down with the Supremes. A loud cheer goes up as the next record, "Back in My Arms Again," is recognized. You feel good watching the niggers get down.

Find Vaughan in the kitchen. His back is against the refrigerator. He's holding his brim and his drink with one hand and a cigarette in the other, leaning his face into some broad. He whispers in her ear loud enough for you to hear him excuse himself. He uncrosses his legs and puts his arms around your shoulder.

"Wanna get off again?" He takes you through the hall and leads you to the bathroom before you can answer.

"Goat, here's some wine, baby," says Spider, grabbing you just as you turn the corner with Vaughan.

Vaughan closes the door, locks it, takes another envelope from his socks.

You are swayed: first by the music, then by the difficulty of saying no now that you are in the bathroom with Vaughan, then by the strange attraction this powder has for you despite the fact it just made you sick a few hours ago. Sniff once, twice up each nostril. You begin to feel it already. Your forehead expands. Vaughan takes three draws, begins to go into some out-of-the-way shit about how this broad wants to take him home. You smile, nod, squeeze past him and the sink, unlock the door, stumble through the hall and into the living room. You forgot your wine. Go back. Vaughan has left. Reenter the living room.

You start rising toward the ceiling. Giggle. Put your hands on your head to keep from hitting it on the ceiling. Dancers' arms and hands float through the air with you. You hope your legs don't go out from under you as you rise toward the ceiling. How come nobody has noticed you're floating up? Bodies bump against you. Some smile, some frown as they get their steps together.

Suddenly you are lifted on a rug and the rug is drifting through the air and banging against clouds. Clouds softer than pillows are hitting you in your head. *Wo oh wo oh wo. . . You've lost that lovin' feeling...wo oh wo oh wo...she's gone, gone, gone ...wo oh wo...*Here's a fine momma bumping against you. You ask her to dance. You stun yourself. You actually are dancing, something you ain't done at a party. *So you're the Goat? I heard a lot about you...how's that little boy of yours?... yeah, known Veralda for a long time...really? ...oh, stop it, you ought to stop it really ...well thank you...*

... People say I'm the life of the party...Oh, I saw Smokey at the Apollo...he was smokin', you know...Oh, stop it, Goat...sure I'm serious, you can come see me...Nowhere to run, nowhere to hide. You're dancing fast now to the Vandellas...hell, the jerk ain't so bad after all...loosen up, roll your head around, shake your shoulders...flap your arms...Gotdam you feel good...clouds going by you ...*I've got sunshine, on a cloudy day*...Another jerk record, huh? ...Temps? ...hey, wait a minute...your stomach again. Somebody has slapped you in the face, kicked you in the stomach. Jerks, spasms. You're on your knees. Your stomach keeps heaving. Spider and Vaughan help you up.

"What's matter with Goat? He sick?"

"Who's that on the floor?"

"Watch out, don't walk in it."

Your eyes are closing; you can feel the red in them. Arms lift your shoulders to the door and out to the elevator. "I'm all right, everything's cool," you protest. You keep saying that everything's cool. Then you are leaning against the chrome bar in the elevator, stepping onto the lobby floor, are walking along the drive toward downtown. You keep saying that everything's cool.

"Goat, are you all right? You all right, my man?" Lead balls are jumping in your stomach. You swear you'll never touch that shit again. "Damn, I didn't know the shit would be faulty, you know? Tell him, Vaughan, it don't usually be that bad." Just get to bed. Turn up Riverside Drive to Ninety-Fifth Street. "You all right now, okay? We gon' cut out, okay?" Take one step into the door and brace yourself against the wall. It's leaning away from you. Get to your room by lunging for the knob as if you were diving. Get your key out. Open into the darkness, fall on the bed with the door still cracked but too far away from you now to reach and promise yourself that you will never ever touch that shit again. Heroin. That shit will kill you. You don't ever want to see that shit again.

10

It's the end of the season. Everybody's here. Kids sitting just out of bounds with their new Afro hairstyles, knee socks, sneaks, backs against the new fence put up this summer. Behind the fence are new stands, and they are jam-packed. Serious basketball watchers are out there in caps, straw hats, Banlon knits, tennis caps. Women and men, children, a few dogs. The Rucker Tournament has almost gone big time now. You look at the white ref in his striped shirt talking to a kid at the sideline. You're dribbling the ball, chewing gum, moving around the basket, bumping into other players during the warmup.

You want to do something big in this last game. You'll be off to college in a few weeks. Rucker Pros just beat Espanade, now college players get ready to take the court. Look around. Fire a jumper. Yvette and Darrin are in a corner to the right of the basket.

You hear somebody talking about the game last week at Mount Morris Park. This dude you saw for Winston Salem when you were at Laurinburg, Earl the Pearl, came up with a team from Philadelphia. Cat who's telling the story is flashing his hands back and forth, describing the action. Says on the first play this dude Earl Monroe dribbles down court, sets up, spins and twirls, dribbling. Whole stadium is lost by his magic. Ball disappears. Cat who's telling this story raises his voice: "The motherfucker disappears, do you hear me? Disappears!" Next thing is the ball has been passed through the middle, past Alcindor even. Dude Alcindor is guarding at center lays the ball up. People are baffled. How did the ball get there? "Motherfuckers couldn't believe it!" Cat who's telling the story stands now and looks down at the fellow he's talking to. Fellow who's listening smiles. You smile to yourself as you get a rebound and go up for a two-handed slammer. Now he's imitating how the Pearl swirled: Cat spins in a circle himself. "So then the whole side of the park filled with these niggers from Philadelphia eating chicken and drinking Kool Aid—whole bus load of them—erupts into one loud voice. They go, 'Black Jesus!'" You listen to the cat say that he was scared, thought a fight might break out or something the way they all shouted like that. So home team gets the ball and they go straight to Lew. Something has to be done to offset the shit that Monroe has pulled. Lew is a low post; backs up, holding the ball high as if he's going to hook, then spins inward toward the middle of the lane and slams it through the nets. "It was the hardest dunk I have ever seen in my life. I swear. The motherfucker was totally unstoppable. Totally. But here's the shit. Lew stuffed it so hard that the God damned ball hit the ground and *bounced over the Mount Morris Park fence!*" Cat's arms go over his head to show how the ball went over the fence. "Then the New York side erupts in a roar that goes, 'The Lord!'"

So take off another rebound and dunk it yourself. How they love the dunk, you think. If there were another way to dunk it, you sure would like to find out. You'd be famous. Here comes Motorman. He's got a red tam and red short sleeve shirt and his megaphone and a big portable radio. He stands on the sidelines and does a few steps to "Papa's Got a Brand New Bag." Behind him are the housing projects, looking like cement towers, reaching into the sky. All these people on this Saturday. You wonder what people do with their lives. Here's Motorman, supposed to have had some smarts, still fucking around in the streets. You hear Carmen is doing okay. What is the difference between the two of them? Maybe it's what Mister Rucker said to you a long time ago. You got to take advantage of your abilities. Motorman should be on his way to studying law or some shit. Now you've got a son being held by his mother over there. What's he going to do? What are you doing with your own life? You know Chamberlain is getting over a hundred thousand dollars. Wonder what you'll make if anything? All these people out here watching you and convincing you that you can make it; do they really know what they talking about? Crazy-assed Spider with his heroin; what is he doing? Hell, play ball now.

Jimmy Walker from Laurinburg and Dexter Westbrook too from Laurinburg are out today. Both playing up at Providence College. Jimmy says it's cold as hell up there, lots of crazy whiteys. Play is swift as usual. Run down court on a fast break— Walker always looks the other way when he passes so you don't expect to intercept the pass. He's smooth too: glides with the ball, but not as well as Pablo, three inches shorter than you and able to throw a whole team off balance. Reminds you of that dude Monroe the way he dips his head and spins. Big dudes Vaughan Harper from Syracuse and Barry White from Hofstra are out too. "Check your man, check your man"—it's Bobby Hunter, easily a clown if given a chance, but always serious on court. Pee Wee Kirkland, goes to school somewhere in the South—you're not sure (Virginia State?)—always got money on him. Race up and race back. Constant up and back movement. Passes zing down and across court. Somebody stops, pumps for his team, you run back. Your team has the ball, you lay back, move around your man although he holds your wrist, shake loose, go up for easy pop. "All right, it's the Goat." Trap your man on surprise press. He loses control and runs into the crowd which scatters against the fence; somebody's jug of iced tea is knocked over; you move to the right then turn so suddenly you surprise yourself and are going to the left across the foul lane, then swing your left hand around in an arc and slam the ball through, leave it trickling along the support post, now padded. You can remember when a kid from high school drove for a lay-up and ran right into the pole, fractured his head or something. Take a man to the base line, pop it in. Pass between three people. Bounce pass at the top of your dribble, where they expect the ball to hit the ground again but instead you whip it through a pack of players. Somebody's always got his hands on you as you go through, switch, stand back then move out again. Swing pass; you got it. Somebody fouls you, you try the old miss play but dude standing at far end doesn't get rebound. "Pick left, pick left." Everybody shoots jumpers. Picks are hard and rough. Once you take the ball into the middle with men on both sides, your back to them, then fade backward and shoot a line drive that just grazes the rim. Move as if you're gliding. Coast to the sides then cut back to the middle. Stay in the air.

You're playing well. The game goes well too. A few spectacular plays—passes and fakes—have pleased the crowd, but you're still thinking there's something about the dunk ... if you could just do something different.

Watching Vaughan's timing on his throwdown, you see a few seconds left over that he hasn't used. This extra time...this extra time...the ball goes through the net but then...

You try on a fast break. One dude is back. You can feel everybody on the sides stand up to watch your move. Never can tell what he may do with an opportunity like this—that's what they're thinking. It's quiet except for the dribbling ball you take down the side with your man swinging at the space between your arms. The patient rhythm of the ball against the cement suddenly changes to a quickening patter as you speed up and drive. Switch the ball to your left hand as you move now so your body is sideways to the bucket. He's in front, protecting the basket. You head fake once, twice, then give him a knee fake and rise. He's lost, stumbling against the pole, like an ice skater losing balance and falling backward. Your arms extend straight upward and you jam the ball down through the nets, and loving the sound of the ball slicing the strings, squint. But you don't let the ball fall trickling to the cement only to roll out of bounds. Instead you *catch the ball with your left hand, place it into your right, bring it back around to the top of the basket and jam it through again. Then your feet touch the ground.*

"Wow...Did you see it? ....Did you see that...My God...I don't believe it...What? ...No, couldn't be...He didn't...Oh, no..."

Hats, beer cans fly in the air. The game is stopped. Kids hug you. Motorman is on his megaphone and announcing what he calls the double throwdown or double dunk, but he is outdone by the pandemonium on the court. You wanted to do something they'd remember you by. You have to smile. You know it's some kind of genius to even think of a shot like that. Nobody has seen *anybody* do *anything* like that, they keep telling you. Where?... how? ...when? ...Dunking the ball twice in one motion while in the air. You know nobody will ever forget that. Yvette has a wide smile on her face when you catch her eyes between the crowd of shoulders and necks. A double throwdown—a shot you yourself own. Okay, so you did it. "A motherfuckin' double dunk," somebody says, "that shit's like walkin' on air."

11

Once again it's time to say goodbye. Some of the trees in Mount Morris Park are already losing their leaves. September. Going to college. Johnson C. Smith. It's a rainy, windy Saturday as you walk on Lenox Avenue. A kid runs across the slick street to the sidewalk with his eyes screwed up to keep out the rain. Lenox is dark gray and wet, with umbrellas dashing past. He turns his head to wave at you and keeps going, but not before you notice the thick ink letters on the side treads of his sneaks: LIL GOAT. You smile. All kinds of people are counting on you.

"Mister Manigault." You turn, lift up your neck in the light drizzle to see who it is. Miss Helen, who owns the candy store. She's leaning out the doorway with her hands over her hair. Her index finger signals you to come to the doorway.

"Whatcha like for today? Give me something good." Feet slosh past you.

"I don't like nuthin'," you say.

"You think a two might lead?"

"I don't know, it might."

"I played a four to lead yesterday, then played a four-nineteen and just missed. It was four-twenty. Come on, give me something good. How your mother doing?"

"She okay. I don't really like nothing."

"Earl gone to college tomorrow," she says, turning to a customer. "But he won't give me a number to play before he go." They laugh. She smiles, the white apron around her large drooping chest rising with her intakes. "Here something for you," handing now from behind the counter a carton of cigarettes. "You study hard now, you hear?" You promise, then duck out into the drizzle again.

Two high school kids stop you, pull you over to a wall which is shelter from the rain. They wish you good luck, joke about some player, ask you about your head fake. Farther down the street three younger kids are throwing a slippery basketball into a tin garbage can. Two other kids are substitutes and stand under the safety of a door ledge, then run out to the sidewalk and play when the others get too wet. You interrupt one of the players to tell him to dribble the ball with his wrist and to stop slapping at it.

These are warm, tender people who stop you on the street and ask about you. They don't even know what it's like to try to hurt somebody. And then you got all that shit going down in the South that you see on television. Niggers getting shot at because they want to go to a school or a restaurant or a movie. You see the shit Martin Luther King is going through in Alabama. At Laurinburg, you all had to sit in the balcony when you went to the movies. You don't understand it. And here these kids are out here playing ball in the rain and people don't want to give them a chance because they are black. They ain't hurt nobody. Then you got these crazy dope addicts running around and stealing from their own people. The parks are dangerous at night. Don't nobody go in them—better not, your head be all whipped up.

You don't want to leave these people and yet you do. It's like going away from a family, and you haven't seen your own in years. Whenever you get back to the Apple from wherever you are, you walk the streets to say hello to all the people in the stores, on the corners, in the park. You like being around them, listening to their laughter, their voices, watching the way they stand in the street, dance without knowing they are dancing, flutter their hands to help conversation. But you want to leave the rest of the city—the noise, cops, hoodlums, pain, poor niggers, worthless niggers—you don't want to see this shit every day.

So this is it, you're thinking. All you got to do is go to class and stay cool, play good ball, and the world is yours. You think you are the best young basketball player in the city of New York. That ain't nothing to sneeze at. You can't miss. It's so simple you can't believe it. You watch guys in the pros on television and you know you can do the same thing. Remember what Rucker said to you, three, four years ago—take advantage of your talent. Goat, you on your way. Smile to yourself.

These goodbyes seems to be the longest of any you've had to make. Your mother always manages to keep from crying. Her smile at times surprises you. Your boys don't make a big thing of it, although Rudy and Bob and you have a goodbye drink in Tillie's. Yvette tries to tell you this is the best way it could have worked out and that she'd rather stay home and take care of the baby anyway, but when she says these words, her cheeks and eyes make movements that tell you she's forcing it out. She's being strong about it, you know. But your mother is aging and now there is a responsibility, a son to consider, and so the leaving has an imprint on you that it didn't have when you went to Laurinburg. It means so much more than it did then. You aren't getting younger. Chamberlain is making over a hundred thousand dollars, Goat. You got to make the right move.

The backboard in the little square across the street there reminds you of the first time you jumped up to grab a quarter from the top of the white metal. A group of you stood around and looked up, just jiving around. Somebody said something about there's a quarter up there and ran toward the dorm to get a ladder. You walked backward four, five steps, leaped forward and snatched the quarter from the top of the backboard. Everybody at Laurinburg was talking about you then.

Well, you make them all—the goodbyes—and again take the two suitcases given you by Mister Burns. This time you ride to the station by yourself. Get on a bus going to Charlotte. You don't sleep the entire way. Just thinking, looking out the window and not really seeing any of the billboards and cars and meadows passing by your eyes. How similar will this be to Laurinburg? You wonder. Will their gym be like a barn too? Will the ground be red clay? Cockroaches in the dorms? Will somebody on the staff make white lightning and sell it to the students in mayonnaise jars?

The bus pulls in with a jerk so hard you almost fall out of your seat. The station is run over with students, but there's a welcoming group from Johnson C. Smith and they know you're coming. They take your bags and direct you to the bus that will transport you to campus. WELCOME JCS FRESHMEN is on one banner. Freshman? Just beginning your college career at twenty-one. Look at these kids, teenagers acting just like you used to act in high school. They look scared as hell too. Asking silly questions. How the hell do you know what you'll major in? Yeah, you think Manhattan is an exciting place to live. Far out.

At the campus you meet the coach and a couple of the players. He's a big dude, heavier than Muffin even, with a way of looking down at you as if he's tumbling backward. Rick Williams. Sounds like a ballplayer's name all right. Something about him though. Although he smiles and shakes his head a lot and seems friendly, you feel just a little uneasy. He walks as if he's on stilts and about to lose his balance.

Then at practice in October you begin to think he cares more about a bunch of pet players than he does about winning. You write to say to Yvette that nobody on the team is even half as good as you, and you aren't bragging. But he designs plays away from you. The first time you jammed the ball there was a split second of awed silence. Even Rick Williams himself scratched his head; you caught him. From then on out you could see he wasn't going to dig you. "Now remember, fellas," he'd say, about to fall backwards with his hands on his hips, "this is teamwork, organized ball, not schoolyard glory-seeking." Then he'd look at you. "Let's play fundamental ball," he'd say every time you passed behind your back or left your man to come over to block another's shot. "Slow it down, slow it down. Set up the shot now." You have nightmares at night in your single room thinking about the day's practice and the ways he could slow you down or make it seem as if you were show-timing. "Pass the ball, pass the ball, don't be greedy." After midnight some morning you jump up in the bed trying to pass the ball.

Classes are ass-kickers. World civilization, English, sociology, math. Almost seems as if you're in high school again by the names of the courses. But Yvette is not here. You squirm in your seat at nights without her aid. How can you read all those pages in one night, do all those math problems, write all those themes? Papers with your essays are returned with so many red pencil marks you can't find what you wrote originally. The words in the books are long things that send you to the dictionary every five minutes. Then you got to re-read the damn paragraph. By midnight you are so sleepy, and this is bad news because you haven't finished half of your assignments.

"You can't explain nationalism, Mister Manigault? We just discussed it at length on Wednesday, and the reading assignment due for last week covered nationalism," says the professor. You twist in your seat, utter something that is quickly ignored. The feet of the other students shuffle in the silence lasting long enough for you to think that everybody is bored with you.

The lectures in sociology go on about mores and some kind of distinctions—individual or invidious, you can't even pronounce it. And as people in the large, dusty hall with windows reaching almost to the ceiling scratch on their pads, you wonder what it is they are taking notes about. One exam asks you to discuss cultural change and its relationship to class structure. You sit there daydreaming and scribbling something—you don't even know what you're writing. What is going on here? The sounds and rhythms don't jive with those sounds you've been hearing. This world seems to be speeding by you. You go to class, sit, wonder. Others are asking questions, arguing, taking all these notes, rushing to the library, staying up all night. Sure there's that group who lollilag, playing cards until morning, drinking wine, sneaking over to the women's dorm. But you've had enough of that. You're serious. You know you can't blow it this time. There's definitely too much at stake.

You write to Yvette on the weekends when you sit in your room. Here you are with the woman you love hundreds of miles away from you. Your son too, and you can't even concentrate on the confusion in this place long enough to guess at how it must be dealt with. You don't have enough money to get back to New York until Thanksgiving. You don't like any of these women, most of them high yellow with long hair and think they cute. *I miss you so much, you know,* you write. *I wish you were just here with me. I could use your help with these books and I want to hold you at night.* Strength is what you need, especially when everything looks as if it's going just fine for all the others. Nobody has any problems as heavy as yours. Look at them anytime—whether it's in the library, cafeteria, walking across the green, even sitting in their rooms—and they have contentment sweeping their faces. You hate to watch the dudes holding their girls around the waist.

One Sunday in October you sit in and write five letters to Yvette. You forget to say things and—sitting and watching some dudes playing football on the lawn just as you sat in your room in Laurinburg, except then it was before Darrin was born and you were worried about getting kicked out— you start a new letter so you can add what comes to you while staring out the window. Thank God for the radio. Yeah, but then they play something like "Tracks of My Tears" by Smokey and you start pacing your room. *Deep inside I'm blue.* Hands in your pockets, walking back and forth over the little scatter rug. *I need you. I need you ... ne-ed You-uh.* You don't really want to hear Smokey, but you can't turn it off. He makes you feel sad, yet you want to feel sad, Goat.

Then to top it off, what you came here for ain't working out. Rick's got all these punk pets he wants to play. You score 27 points in the first game and then he doesn't play you for the *next three.* If that ain't madness, what is?

"Everything's cool, young man. You're an asset to the team. A real contribution."

"But, I'm not playing regularly," you say, frowning, you're so damned confused. "Why aren't I?"

"You're playing," about to tilt forward, he insists. "Don't worry yourself. You're playing."

'I'm sitting down, I'm not playing." This is his office one day, on his grounds, so you feel like the intruder. He can put you out or end the conversation any time he wants. It's not like you two were in the dormitory or something like that. No, you're on his turf. "I came here to go to school and play ball, but I'm not playing."

"You're playing. Everything's all right."

You guess maybe he doesn't understand English. You are not playing. You know that. You know when you are sitting on the bench. You aren't that dumb. You don't have amnesia and shit. So how can you argue against some shit like that? You write Yvette, but she has no answer for this. You say you ain't playing, he says you are. You aren't. Crazy.

So crazy he's got your name fucked up a little. Dudes drop your passes. Motherfuckers don't screen or set simple picks. You make four jumpers in a row and he pulls your ass out, talking about, "cool off." Snatch rebounds away from opposing centers and he wants you to lay back instead for the fast break. You dribble too much. You don't pass enough. You take wild shots. You show-time. Then after he sits you on the bench and gets you mad as hell, you have to go back in, and you so upset you throw the ball away. Then he pulls you. Fuck that. You know how good you are. You haven't seen a player yet in all the games you've played by Christmas who's half as good. What's he trying to prove? You don't run around talking about yourself, but you know how good you are.

By February you are really fed up with it all. Your grades are disastrous. You fail English and sociology, just pass math and take an incomplete in world civilization. You out-play everybody when you get in the game, but he hardly lets you stay. You could have gone to UCLA, you tell yourself. Here you are with some jive nigger country coach who tells you everything's all right and you're playing when you ain't playing and therefore ain't nothing right. Soon as the season's over you'll get your hat, you promise yourself one day while looking out the window. Fuck exams, just get your hat.

The clincher is when you overhear him talking about you one day. He's walking down the hallway after practice and you know it's his voice. You're running a towel over your shoulders in the locker room. He calls you a troublemaker.

You win the last game and everybody's happy. You played the whole second half but weren't even thinking about basketball. Still you scored fifteen points. The team's yelling and shouting and punching each other in the locker room. Wilbur, one of the pets, shakes a Pepsi Cola bottle up and gets ready to squirt the soda at you. "I'll kick your fucking ass if you do," you say. Towels are dropped by players undressing across from you. Bodies coming out of the shower stop short. Wilbur has a grinning frown on his face. He isn't shaking the soda anymore. You turn your back to him and get dressed. There's a slow buzz of talk, a murmuring that erupts into loud voices when you slam the door to the locker room. Walk down the hall of lockers, gray steel just like Benjamin Franklin, and out the door. Go to your room where your bags are already packed. Fuck them. You haven't really figured the shit out. You never felt as if you adjusted to the academic shit. And you can't figure out why that country nigger didn't like you. You aren't even sure you're doing the right thing by leaving. But you're nobody's sucker, that's a bet. Believe that. Get your hat. Leave this shit. Go home.

12

Who was the dude who said shit never goes right in March? You do remember Rudy talking about the Ides of March. The riot in Madison Square Garden. Holcomb Rucker died. And now the Goat returns to New York. Supposed to be in school studying and shit and making all-American or Little All American or something like that. Inventor of the double dunk. Scholarships to 73 colleges including UCLA, where Lew is. Baddest dude in the city. Got a son to take care of too. Wilt Chamberlain making over a hundred thousand dollars and you figure you should be worth that much in four years and look at you now. Back in Port Authority. Motherfuckers pushing you around like you some ordinary nigger. And you are. Had a chance to get started on the big road ... what ... it was too much pressure ... couldn't handle the books ... coach didn't like you ... what? ... what? ... what ... ?

Hop in a cab after standing outside the station for almost a half hour. Nobody wants to drive to Harlem in the evenings. You don't blame them. Mad as you are, you'd like to knock somebody on his ass just on GP. Your stomach is so weak your muscles are jumping. You can't remember when you've felt so Gotdam bad. Just bad, that's all. Don't want to hear no music, don't want to talk, don't want to do nothing. Nothing. Mutha-fuckin' motherfuckers. Aw shit, Goat. Look at the splendid shit on Broadway. Fur coats. Big rides; you mean Mercedes and Jags and Rolls; not just Cadillacs. People are making it big, all over Broadway. Look at them living it up; happy and shit. Having big fun. You don't even have any gloves.

"Right here, right here!"

"Hold it, my man, can't you read the fuckin' numbers?" He must think you live on Riverside Drive or some shit the way he zooming by your crib. He's gonna stay right here and let you walk back three doors, huh? Well, you ain't movin' until he backs up to let you out directly in front of your crib. Just sit here. "I don't live here, man." He looks at you in the mirror. "I said three-thirty six. This ain't it, you know?" Half laugh, half snarl. "You can back up or I'll get out and not pay." You're thinking about doing that anyway.

"Okay," he sighs and sucks his teeth, but puts the cab in reverse. Here you are returning to a motherfucker you aren't supposed to see until June and you have to put up with ignorant white-boy-cab-driver-shit soon's you arrive. You ought to punch him in his pimply mug.

Thank God it's too cold for anybody to be out on the damn street. That's all you need is a welcoming party. Your bags bang against your thighs as you hustle across Ninety-Fifth Street to the hotel. Your hands have already stiffened in the half minute it takes you to get to the door. Snot flows from your nose and the Hawk whips up the street from Riverside Drive and crawls down your neck. Pull on the metal doorknob. Steam hisses from the long radiator in the hall. The two bulbs in the ceiling are spotted with insects. A head and shoulder peek around the hallway at the end.

"Who it is?" The eyeglasses sparkle.

You don't say anything, just keep walking, knowing she'll recognize you. The figure comes out in the open, stands now in head scarf and robe in the middle of the hallway.

"Earl?'

You sigh, "Yeah, hi," drop your bags as she comes to hug you.

"What you doin' here?"

"I left."

"Left?" She moves back, "Left where, how? ... for what? ... when? ..."

You lean against the wall and are overtaken by a flood of defeat and disappointment. You bend your neck and start crying. Now you're babbling, making no sense at all and unable to stop it as you hear your voice running and bouncing down the hall and off the ceiling. *No good, no good ... they didn't want me there ... the work was too hard ... I tried ... wouldn't let me play ... aw, Mom, I tried, I tried.*

"Come on, I still got your room for you," grabbing your shoulder and one of your bags, she escorts you back down the hall. "I know you tried. The Lord didn't mean for it, that's all. You get some rest." She turns on the light for you, folds back your blanket, sits in the chair that creaks.

Sit on the comfortable bed, the most comfortable bed in the world; your bed, your mattress, the familiar give of the springs. Your mother sits in the corner. You thought she was going to pitch a bitch. You wanted her to. You wanted her to tell you to come here, like the day you ran away from her, and you wanted her to slap you in the face and shake your shoulders so your head would jerk back and forth on your neck. You wanted her voice to screech names in your ear, names like *no-good nothing, worthless bum, trifling so-and-so.* Oh, please, Mom, oh please do something to me, make me see what it is I don't see. Hurt me as you are hurt sitting there in the creaky chair and telling me that whatever I do, whatever I do, I am your son and you will always support me.

Now she twists in her seat and leans to the side and runs her hand under the apron and pulls out her handkerchief and pats her forehead, saying, "Hot in this room. You won't need a blanket, Earl."

Then she dabs at her nose and starts blinking her eyes. You want to go over and put your head in her lap and press your head into the white, wrinkled apron and then climb up on her lap until your head is all the way in and then your shoulders and chest are too and soon you could get all of your body into the warm, white hollow of her apron. Nobody could ever bother you there. Ball yourself up and go to sleep in her apron.

"I don't know," she says. "He works in mysterious ways. Wonders to unfold."

"I tried, Mom, I tried," you say.

"Lord didn't mean for it that way. What will be, will be. Get you some rest, boy. Everything gonna be fine." She leans toward you as she struggles out of the chair, and walks past you with heaviness, her hips plump where the apron string is drawn tightly around her body. She is out of the door quietly and is soon humming, "Rock of Ages" as she scrapes down the hallway.

Alone now to examine designs in the floor, you cup your palms to hold your forehead as you stare down. Take a nap on your back, then rise later, around 11, and get into the street where you can drown these disappointments. But rest now, *rest...*

The coach points a finger at you after you have driven and dunked the ball. Everybody behind him is laughing. The finger is thicker than a pipe. Everybody is laughing. The finger is on your nose tip. He says that nobody is allowed to dunk and that you shouldn't. He wants you to undunk the ball. From behind him one of his pets appears to hand you a ball. Everybody is waiting. You have the ball and everybody is waiting.

Wake up with trembling fingers and the scary realization that nobody is watching you. You are on the bed in this room in this darkness by yourself.

You don't care how cold it is outside, you don't want to sit here. Get out. You want to see the baby but not tonight. Yvette's old man will give you that look and Yvette herself will be startled. All the explaining: you're not hardly ready for that right now.

So brush your hair after you empty your bags, throw on your jacket and turn the doorknob. Tell your mother that you'll see her in the morning.

"You gon' to see Yvette this time of the night? You got money?"

Tell her that you might. Outside, you frown at the cold. Lick your lips to keep them from getting chapped. Bend your head. Where to? Uptown. Steam comes out of the manhole. Cabs and private cars rattle down West End. You walk up to the lights of Broadway, passing the Thalia where you sat and hurt your eyes trying to read the subtitles to a foreign film; back hunched, fists in pants pockets, you glance at the Chinese laundry; then the Symphony and the all-night newsstand and the all-night luncheonette and the bright lights of Broadway. The subway rumbles under your feet. Run across the street to catch the cab that is discharging a passenger smoking a pipe.

Direct him to One-Twenty-Fifth and stop him at St. Nicholas, just before Eighth. Jump out and walk over to the projects. A couple of dudes huddle together on the corner, turn to cheek you out and go back to their business. You hustle up the walkway to the wide metal door, then take the steps two at a time, swinging on the metal banisters when you turn at the landings. Bang on the door. You hear a stereo. It's Stevie Wonder. The door unclicks: *Upright, everything is all right.* Rush opens the door. He's in a black-and-white dashiki.

Big smile: "Goat. Gotdamn. Come on in. Come on it. Watcha doing in town, semester break or something?" He gives you the power handshake. Your coat is in his hands, you're in the living room. Three dudes sit on the coach straight ahead. You nod at the familiar faces.

"Naw, I left, man."

"Left? What happened?" He's shorter than you, and stands in the middle of the room, his head cocked to the side and his arms outstretched. Momentarily you think he's jiving you. He looks like one of those sea gulls hovering. He thinks bad news is about to come and can't wait, yet pretending he cares. Plus you know the other dudes are duds, failures, has-beens. They don't care if you make it or not. Probably be happier if you didn't, shit. Well, maybe you're wrong.

"Aw, man, I couldn't deal with that shit. Coach didn't like me, wouldn't let me play."

One dude from the couch responds: "Wouldn't let *you* play?" He looks at the other two dudes for agreement. "He got to be crazy. Wouldn't let *the Goat* play?" They snort with disgust.

You're sitting in a stuffed chair now and facing them. Rush is to your right, in another chair.

"Hey man look, whatcha got? I have a few bucks, you know," going into your pocket.

"Goat, this is me. Put your money away," says Rush. "You wanna do some coke or sniff some heroin?"

"Hey man, I'm down, you know. I'm really in the dumps. Let me have some heroin."

He moves fast. The stereo to your left hosts the Four Tops. You like it: "Reach Out, I'll Be There." You all move closer together to the center of the floor on the rug. The windows on the wall that the stereo is against are all steamed up. Bend over, take a swift snort, drawing granules of snow through the stick. Then sit back. Pretty soon you're talking your ass off. You're talking much more than you had planned: about the school, the funny rules, the bust in the girls' dorm. How you jumped so high you kicked a dude in the mouth. They fill you in on shit that has gone down in the Apple. You smile, nod your head. Clouds bump into you again; your feet go up in the air. Their faces bang into each other. Life is wonderful again; it's beautiful. Everything is beautiful. Colors, sounds. It's all so clear now. They talk about Malcolm X and although you haven't heard the brother, you understand everything they say he has put down. Absolutely. Um hum. Of course. You even elaborate on a few of his theories, expand with an illustration or two. You rap with them and are amazed at yourself that you can hold your own. Nothing can confuse you now. Everything's bright, distinct. Keep talking, you love it.

The music too is so much clearer. You can hear everything: the tambourines in "I'll Be There" sound so real; the horns in 'Papa's Got a Brand New Bag" are on the money.

You don't know how long you have been there when you feel your eyelids drooping heavily. Your head begins to fall to your chest. In a daze you see the other fellows twisting into their overcoats. Rush is saying something about the sofa pulls out, and in half-dream and half-stumble, you are falling on it and burying your head into the pillows.

Your dreams are funny and filled with extraordinary happenings. Cats flying in the air, dogs running backward. You awake laughing and feeling as if you've hardly slept at all. Outside the steamed window is the beginning of the gray day. Rush's bedroom door is closed. You go to the bathroom, rinse out your mouth, take a shower, put on your clothes, tip back into the living room, check the kitchen and drink half of the quart of orange juice in the refrigerator.

Smile at all the crayoned signs in the landings as you go down the steps. Outside, the day begins. People wait for buses and hustle to subways. Another cold-as-hell day. What to do? Walk up One-Hundred Twenty-Fifth, your hands in your pockets and thinking. Get on the subway and go to the Bronx. You can't face Yvette right now, no way. What can you say? How can you say it? Here, stop in this cafeteria for some eggs and grits and bacon and coffee. It's filled with old people reading folded newspapers and dressed in yesterday's style. All the dudes wear hats and have no teeth. All the women have thick red lips. They aren't any happier than you are. What is it about life that fucks with you? Why are these people and you so damned out of it? Did they have coaches who fucked with them, school principals who fucked with them? Or did they fuck themselves up? Was it something they did or was it already planned for them? Aw, shit, get out of here and run up the street for the subway.

At One-Hundred Sixty-First you get off with all the old white-haired Jews and hustle down the hill to Jerome Avenue. You walk through the park eclipsed by Yankee Stadium. At the gym door you see Romeo. You start to turn around but he sees you, waves you over. He's standing with his hands in his pockets and jumping around in a small circle to keep warm. He's lost weight. His eyes are smaller, red, weak-looking. He's lost weight, you notice again: his tan cashmere coat is like a robe on his body. "What happened?" he asks finally after you can't go through any more small bullshit conversation. You tell him, flapping your arms against your legs to keep warm, squinting your eyes. He looks hurt. "Damn Goat, I'm sorry to hear that shit, man." He turns away from you for an instant and in that moment neither of you say anything; a time to review your lives secretly. Two blocks away the IRT subway rattles in the air above you. "Wanda left me, you know. Took all my money and split to Philly." He's still not facing you but looking beyond the neat, high-rent buildings on Jerome Avenue to the roofs farther into the High bridge section of the Bronx. He's looking for Wanda, you think. "Les tip, bro." You huddle your shoulders up, stuff your hands into your pockets and go down the walkway to the sidewalk.

"Anybody in there?" you ask.

"Some high school chumps, you know. Ain't nobody close to the shit you used to do at Franklin, man. Goat, I'm on the shit," he says, and for the first time you notice the honk in his voice. His eyes are red.

"Yeah, I heard. I saw Rush last night."

"You know Jim-Jim from down the valley—he o-deed, Goat. Dude had a bad defensive game, man. Penn was looking at his ass, he was all-city," throwing up his hands, "and then putz. Shit's killing off your brothers like flies, Goat. Like muthafuckin' flies. Blip, blip, blip—just like that."

Everybody talking about it. You think somebody need to come through Harlem and clean out the whole muthafukah, burn it down and start all over again. Naw, that wouldn't do shit. Brothers and sisters look out on the terribleness of the day, the scare of the night, the nothing of it all, the nothing of anything, especially they lives and see nothing. You know this. You know deep down inside you are as scared and confused as all the other brothers. *There ain't nothing to turn to.* Dig it: what is the other choice? Where you gonna go, watcha gonna be?

"I just copped from a dude at the gym. I'm gonna get down. I need this shit like a muthafuckah, Goat. I need it."

Up the steep hill of Anderson Avenue where Romeo used to live, past the library, over to Woodycrest and then Ogden. Somebody's car burglar alarm squeals and three people walking toward you ignore it. A block away are the projects. Romeo hustles ahead. When you reach the entrance, Romeo pushes against the door and you both half-run to the elevator straight ahead and press B. Down in the basement, Romeo skips to the laundry. His hands shake as he crouches down by the line of washing machines. You have closed the door. He pulls out his shit from his overcoat; wine bottle cap, ball of cotton, eye dropper, needle, necktie. "Put some water in the cap for me." He heats it with a match, but his fingers drop it and you go back down to the sink to fill it up again. He puts the match under the cap again, heating the water. Dissolves the white powder in the cap. Places the cotton in the cap. Draws up heroin through the eye dropper. Lets the needle suck out the heroin from the tip of the eye dropper. He pulls up his pants leg and you squint your nose at the purple needle marks dotting his calf. "Tie it tight, Goat." You wrap the faded narrow red tie around his leg, bulging a vein. His hands shake. Romeo eases the needle into his vein, sighs, "ah ... ah ..." A restful, heavenly smile spreads across his mouth, his eyes go blurry. "Come on, you gon' get down, ain't you, blood? Better hurry up."

"I don't want to, man."

"Just take a skin pop. You don't have to go to the vein." You want to be convinced, really. Your world is rapidly dissolving away from you. This is one way of keeping it solid. You want something in your hands, something in your head, something to feel other than the overweight of dejection. Nothing feels good to you but the clouds hitting tenderly against your forehead. You want it, really. Okay, take a skin pop, just let the needle go in your skin. And soon you are beautifully aloft. You hear the Four Tops in your memory, the tambourines shaking in your left ear.

I'llll...be there
to hold you ...I'llll
be there...

Your back is against a washing machine, your legs stretched out straight. Peace. Soft, tender peace. Everything is fine. Uptight, everything is all right. Babee, outasight....People say I'm the life of the party...you've got that lovin' feelin'...nowhere to run, nowhere to hide...float...doze...easy... *"Ohma God! Oh mah God... Help! ...It's dope addicts in here...they're dead... help, I can't move...Oh, Lord, help me...they're dead...hellllp... hellllllllllp...dope addicts! ... helll..."*

Shake your head, What is it? Who is it? A lady shouting at the top of her lungs. Standing in the doorway and shouting at the top of her lungs. You bend forward to get up and as your hands reach forward she screams again and then falls against the door molding and slides down to the floor. Romeo is on his knees and scraping up his shit off the floor. Later you remember he looked like a KO'd boxer. Grab your jacket. Your heart is galloping. What did you do wrong? She screamed, that's all you know. You follow Romeo out. He stops, bends over, and his fingers sprint through her handbag lying at her feet; he takes some bills out of her purse. *Down-here...I heard the scream, sounded like it was from the laundry...Oh, I hope nothing is wrong...it was a woman..."*

Run right toward them. It's a woman and a man. Don't stop. Knock them down. You don't care who they are or anything. They're in your way and you gotta get out of here. She curls up against the wall. *"What's...what's going on here?"* His eyes are big and his lips are trembling before you push his shoulder against the wall.

Outside it has begun to snow. You're running now just a step behind Romeo but slow down when you get several blocks away. Don't look suspicious. Walk normally as the snowflakes fall on your nose. Damn, you wish you hadn't left your gloves on that bus. "Hey, where to, man?" You ask as you walk side by side now.

"My crib up on the Concourse. How do you feel?"

"Hungry, but good, you know."

"It's almost lunch time. We'll grit at my place. Hey, Goat, what happened?"

"This woman started screaming."

"No, I mean to us. You were supposed to go pro. I was supposed to go to art school."

"We'll get it together."

"Yeah?" He looks at you funny, as if he knows something you couldn't possibly understand right now. "This shit has me, man. I can't give it up. The iron lady. The horse. I can't give her up. She got me. Go-ot damn she got me."

Walk the half-dozen blocks to the Concourse. "How you get this crib, man?" You're walking into the lobby. A mirror covers one wall. Carpeting. Two couches. An old lady sits in one with a poodle in her lap.

"Oh, you know, doing different shit."

You know exactly what he's talking about when you walk into his apartment. In his bedroom are two color televisions. Cameras are on the floor by the bed. This is Romeo now, you think. Had a lot of shit going for him. Could draw his ass off, won all the art contests in high school. Everybody knew he would design some bad, bad fashions. Now what, Romeo? What kind of shit could push you into this? Stealing. Stealing to live, you bet. He admits he's hooked. You stand in his bedroom and half see as he opens the closet door to show a dozen suits with the tags hanging from the sleeves. Your heart sinks. Here is what failure means. You couldn't make it in college, couldn't make it legitimately, so you're left with this, right? If you don't make it big the way you're supposed to, as Mister Rucker said, taking advantage of your talent, then you're reduced to this? You mean there's no better way? Goat, you ask yourself, what the fuck are you going to do now that you're in New York? You got a baby to take care of, you got a few bucks, a basketball talent, no job, a high school diploma, and what? ... what? All your boys are in college. The ones that made it. The others don't even count, really, like you won't pretty soon. Here you are back in New York with your man.

Fuck it; you got some time to figure this out. Accept Romeo's invitation to crib with him for a month or so. He has an extra bedroom. Okay, you just need a few days to work things out in your mind, then you'll know where your head's at. Right. Just a few days. Then you'll have a plan for Yvette and the baby and yourself. But right now you need to relax. You see Romeo pulling out the works again. Your heart patters. His muffled stereo drifts from the living room. He puts the dropper and needle and shit on the dresser. You pull off your socks and sit on the bed. You can spend the entire day here getting high and rapping to Romeo about the shit you had to go through in Charlotte.

It's snowing in New York. You've been here for twenty-four hours and now you're just cooling out, getting ready to figure out your next move. It's snowing in New York. Stay inside today and try to straighten out your head. Romeo gives you the tie. As you wrap it around his arm, he starts a story about a party you both went to while in high school. You're looking out his bedroom window across the way where the snow is falling on the fire escape—looking while tying and thinking you'll cook some eggs and bacon and grits after this high. His vein is big as a jump rope.

13

High is so nice. High is so beautiful. You float. Hi, high. Whoever invented this shit should be rewarded. Jesus Christ this shit is good. Look at the clouds; they're so soft and fluffy, bouncing off your head as you glide through the air. You can't help but dunk the ball from way up here in the sky.

You've been away from your moms for a week now. Everytime you think about going back and then checking out Yvette, you get cold feet. Then you get high and you feel too damn good to consider anything serious. Hell, everything's cool. You're just trying to get it together. It's nothing serious, you're just skin-popping, not going to the vein. Now *that* would be some rough shit. Romeo already reduced to stealing cars to keep up his habit. But you'll never get into it that far, no way. No way. This shit is just temporary—absolutely temporary. That shit ain't going into your veins. Your mother would pitch a bitch. You need your legs and arms for the court, baby. No mainlining for your ass.

You haven't been out, just laying dead in Romeo's pad and watching him parade back and forth with shit: radios, fur coats, televisions, typewriters. It's a wonder the dude don't get no hernia and shit. He had you helping him carry a damn stereo and television combination a couple of days ago. It was still in the box so it looked cool, plus it was in the daytime.

Look out the window. You think the weather's going to break soon. Spring. That's the best time to get your head together anyway. Friday. Romeo should get in any minute; it's close to five. Have a late dinner, get high again. You still got time to get your shit together. Maybe by Monday you'll be straight. Yeah. Tell Romeo you'll cut out on Monday. Then you'll have to leave and go back to your moms. Need some clothes anyway. Can't keep washing the same shit over and over.

At seven the rooms get dark. You walk around only half-high to pull down the shades and click on the lights. Sit in the big chair in the living room and listen to the radio. Just cool out. Doze. Wake up an hour later. Romeo's still not here. Go pour yourself some blackberry-flavored brandy, try to keep the high. You know there's no more dope in the crib. Frankie Crocker is cooking tonight, playing all the best jams. You used to call in dedications to Cindy when you were in high school, then listen all night to hear the cut. The brandy puts a mellow glow around you. You listen to Otis Redding's "Try a Little Tenderness" with a dull, floating sensation. You don't want to move. God, the nigger can sing. Oh, you don't want to move. Doze some more. You should start dinner now that it's ... what?—almost nine-thirty? Where the hell is Romeo? You wonder if the nigger got busted. That shit never even occurred to you before. Now you're straightening out. If he is busted, they'll come here and get your ass with all this shit in here. And you laying up high and shit.

Stand up. Your heart races as you go to the window and look down, leaning on the window sill, to the Grand Concourse. You're afraid you might see a half dozen police cars, sirens and whistles and pigs in blue surrounding the building and blocking traffic. No, just the usual hunched backs hustling along the Concourse. Maybe you ought to get out of here. You have overstayed your welcome somewhat. Romeo ain't here. That's the main thing. You don't know what's up. Rush into the bedroom and get your jacket, put on your socks and shoes, go into the kitchen for some potato chips and Pepsi and hustle through the living room and out the front door.

Check your wallet as you walk along the Concourse to the subway. Four bucks. Everybody you know is out of town. Who you gonna borrow bread from? Your moms will give you too much static and you definitely can't go to Yvette now, not after being in town for a week without contacting her. Sit rocking on the subway as you think of what you must do this Friday night. Damn, things are so down and empty inside your stomach. You feel so sad. Think of Otis Redding's "Try a Little Tenderness." *Things may get weary, they often do get weary.* That's what you need, something to bring you out of this sad weariness. The lead in your chin forces you to nod. All these old people sitting on this car are so much happier.

You need it. That's what it's all about, Goat. You need it. It frightens you. You need it. Naw, not like Romeo, stealing cars, stereos and cameras. Waking up with cramps. Going out of his mind, sweating. You don't need it like that. But you are sweating. Your face is hot. You need something to lift you up. Oh, no. Oh, yes. You need it. You clench your fists, uncross your legs, try to breathe normally. You are scared now. Your life is scary. You need it. You're hooked. You know it. You have never had any sensations like this in your life. Who's watching? You've never wanted anything like you want it now. God, you feel so low, so damn low. Only it can lift you up, convince you that smiles and laughter are possible. Oh shit. Oh please, you need it.

Look desperately back now to your boyhood and the sand roads of Charleston. Mommagran telling those big boys from across the tracks to leave you alone. She holding you around the shoulder as you both stand on the porch. This is what you want now—the warm comfort of something ... something to shake this jitteriness, this invisible monster trying to pull you away from Mommagran. Blank white faces are rocking blurs across from you. The subway train pulls your body, then pushes it back, then pulls it, and the white faces stare still. The subway pulls you, the faces stare, your stomach is hollow and you want to retain the vision of your Mommagran holding you.

No. No, she slips away from you like one of those fast players moving around a pick, his waist easing away from your hands. Only it is Mommagran's arm easing away and you are left facing the pain bubbling within you as the blank globes bounce on their necks across from you. You must come up with a solution and feel it, it is so close. Your hands are almost touching it, the magic words, the uplifting secret, the answer is ... is ...

Aunt Hattie. You ain't seen her in years. Aunt Hattie. Hell yes, Aunt Hattie. You can't sit still now, you're so anxious. Your toes twitch. Oh, you can already feel the clouds bouncing off your forehead. Stand, hold on to the turnstile, ready to go. Outside you're smiling as you walk up the avenue toward her apartment. You're only minutes from rescue. She'll save you. Aunt Hattie. Gotdamn, ain't seen her in *years,* Goat.

Funniest thing how the building hasn't changed in years. You remember the evening you arrived in this town. Now again—and you've only visited her about twice since then—you enter the hallway. You stand shivering with anticipation. You glance over the grille of spaces and brass buttons on the wall, then find her name, then walk down the shiny tiles.

She asks who it is when you knock on the door. The door swings open and she's in her stocking cap and robe, big smile of shiny teeth. You collapse into the lumpy chair you used to sleep in.

You have to lie to her. Never in your life have you even conceived of lying to an aunt. All right, you're desperate. Your toes twitch. You hate every word of it, but you give her the story because now it's lie or something else, and you can only describe that something as too, too painful, something you can't bear. And if you can escape it by lying, you will lie.

So you're home for spring vacation but had to borrow the money from the school chaplain to pay for the ticket. In order to pay him back you have to get a job while you're here on vacation. The only way you can get a job is to go to an employment agency. They require a registration fee. Could she please lend you the money so you can pay the fee and get a job in a restaurant so you can pay back the chaplain? Could she also help you in paying for the waiter's pants—they have to be a special wool—you'll need for the job? Also, your return trip...

She asks finally how much you need. You tell her. She frowns, says that you never visit her, she's been sick, nobody telephones her. Only when you want something. You ask her why she never wrote you back. She is stunned. You wrote her a letter? Of course you did. You wanted her to know you were on the honor roll—uh, dean's list. She smiles. Now you ask her about Earlene, the girl who used to baby-sit for you when you were a kid. She's really smiling now, astounded that you remember Earlene. You're getting a pain in your stomach. You're running off at the mouth. You have decided to study to become a doctor. You can't wait to get back to school. What does she think of Malcolm X—isn't he crazy? She gives you the money, going first to her closet, then taking the balled up stocking cap into the bathroom, then emerging. You hug her, tell her you love her, and get your hat. You fly down the steps and out the door.

You know where Romeo goes. You'll try the same place. You got the money to take a cab now. You doing good again. Shit, that was even funny. As you think of how damn good you're going to feel, you start smiling. What a performance. You ought to be shot, Goat. Lying to your aunt like that. You did a job. No shit. You're still grinning as you get out the cab, and almost ignoring the stabs in your chest now because you have the answer for them, the beautiful answer for these pains—walk down the avenue.

You're on Eighth and One Twenty-Sixth. The faces in the doorways move under the moonlight. Down the avenue. A voice whispers something about the black, red, Methadone, Jolly Jamaica, good smoke, hash, big red. People dart all around, through alleys, to cars, from cars, down steps, out of buildings. Elbows and knees are signals. Hand signs and nods are symbols. Shoulders bump into yours, big hats twirl. You stop in a doorway. Small talk, nods. You go into your pocket. He goes into his. Subway roars overhead. Another dude on the sidewalk paces—wide black hat, cupped palms around the flame, mustached smile, the look upward from the cupped flame. Dash into Cadillac, into kitty kat, headlamps on, smoking exhaust pipe. You now stumbling in some hallway. They got the tie around your arm. Bulging vein is purple now and you're smiling your ass off, you're so happy to be this close to the pillows of clouds bouncing off your forehead. Ah...the needle punctures, loosens all muscles. You are free again. Now you go to glide, float upward, haha, giggly giggly looka Earl, mama, looka Earl, haha upsa daisy, upsa daisy ... high again. The clouds bounce against you. You're doing good again. Real good. High. Beautiful.

You are high so much you lose count of the days. You heard some of them talk about stupefication, some of the dudes who been on it for awhile, and you think you have some idea of what they mean. Finally you had to take it in the vein, in the main line, that night Romeo didn't show. Come to find out the nigger got arrested for grand larceny ("Nigger had about three pianos in his apartment," is how the story goes by one claiming he lived in the crib next door) and is serving two-to-ten and be out on probation in the summer. But just in your arms, not your legs, where your jumping ability is. You won't get to the point that some of them have—popping their jugular veins and penises.

All the chicks and dudes you discover on heroin are mostly all the people you knew in school who didn't want to do shit. Now they paying for it, you think, just as you are. Don't do shit, won't be shit, somebody used to say. Free schools and dumb niggers.

Pay a few bucks to use somebody's shooting gallery and you see them all down there. You got your own needle now from Harlem Hospital— a nurse who worked there on the night shift copped—for three bucks. So all you have to do is rent the rest of the works. You don't just want any old needle going into your arm, un unh.

It's always in the basement unless you dealing with some real high prices. Always around the furnace where the heat is. You go every morning now, before nine, as if you're going to a gig. Sit on wooden crates or molded mattresses. Go over to the faucet to get the water. Bodies—not faces or individuals or people with working constitutions, but bodies—male and female, line the walls, propped like Raggedy Ann dolls. You have to bend under the heating pipes when you move around. Cobwebs in the corners. About a half-dozen. Sometimes as many as thirty. Teenagers on their way to school. Old ladies with scars on their cheeks. One old hag who couldn't find her vein, she's been doing it for so long. She begs somebody to beat on her arm to make the vein come up. "Kick it if you have to." There's a dude whose leg is swollen with abscesses. They all come to the gallery every day like club members. In the dimly lighted celler, veins pop from necks, arms, legs, dicks. Needles flash. Sighs and moans compose a dull chorus. Snores from some who nod.

The conversations are always out the side of the mouth so as not to lose any energy. Low-keyed. So-and-so has the best shit around this week. Sold four bundles Thursday on Morningside—that's getting to be a hot spot. That nigger in the Riverton with the two stereos ... that candy store on the corner of ... that old man who lives ... they can be taken off by a smart, desperate thief. Get out by noon or you could be in serious trouble. People are desperate. They look at you and at each other with dripping tongues and half-closed eyes. They'll kill you if you tell them you got fifty bucks on your ass. Old dudes who left the gallery to be followed and beaten and robbed by the folks who were sitting next to them. You've seen coats, watches, rings, socks taken off of those who made the mistake of nodding. To wake up and discover you're chilly because someone has stolen your pants is no big thing. The shit is so serious though, nobody laughs at the dude cursing with just his underwear on.

The world has stopped for you as you sit on a squeaking, stained mattress with your head down looking at the dirt floor and these bodies in gray clothes and scarred, drawn faces move around you as if you're in the middle of a merry-go-round. They're there, but it's really only you in the world. Nothing else counts as you float so peacefully through the world which has stopped for you. Fantastic pink clouds tickle your neck. You're doing what you have to do, Goat. You'll get it together sooner or later, but right now ...

Right now you're laying dead, getting yourself together. And it's the pain in the morning that sends you back. Soon's you get rid of these fucking pains, you'll straighten up. But see, you wake up in some friend's pad, some friend who's hooked on the shit, with burning stomach cramps. You got to get out and take care of these cramps. Your arms and legs ache. You can't breathe right. Stabs of pain zig-zag through your chest and down to your stomach. You got to get out and make it to the gallery.

Before you know it, it's April, warm. Seems like just yesterday you came in from Charlotte. The colors of spring are in little girl's clothes. Convertibles line the avenue. You can smell the trees. Heads are filled with smiles. You ain't been home in months. Goat, what's it mean? You sit scratching your neck one day on a stop and hear one kid in sneakers tell another that you're on the shit. You raise your head (it hurts). Who's that punk talking about? You? You're just getting your shit together—what's he mean, hooked? What's he mean? You stand on the stoop, your arm pointed at him, trying to get his attention so you can straighten his ass out, but you lose your footing and stumble to the sidewalk as you grab on to a parking sign pole. You turn. Heads look out windows, bodies stand in doorways. They're not smiling. They're looking at you. The thought bangs against your head, but you try to ignore what it's saying. Admit it. They know. You ought to know too and stop jiving yourself, nigger. You're hooked. Oh, no. Sit down on the stoop again. Scratch. Think—try to think of what you've been doing these last days, weeks. Events won't stay in your mind. Names and places mean nothing. Oh God, Goat, you're hooked. You know it. Yes, the bitch has gotten your ass. Horse. Big H. Put your face in your hands now. You can feel the tears rolling down your fingers into your palms. Your cheeks twitch. You're hooked, damnit. You're hooked. Okay, straighten up and walk tall. After all, you're the Goat. You don't even have the strength to… who's this?

You squint your eyes, jerk back your neck. The figure, the walk, the hair look too familiar. You remember your face isn't washed. She's not looking in your direction. You ease down the steps with your back to her and start trotting. Gotdamn, you don't want her to see you. Just jog easily, as if you're enjoying the nice spring day.

"Earl?"

Just keep jogging. "Earl ... Earl…"

Dash across the street now without looking. You might even want to get hit by a car before you let her see you. Reaching the sidewalk, you turn your head sideways slightly to see where she is. She's in the middle of the street, cars fanning by her, and her face looks wild and confused, her arms are in the air as if she's losing her balance. For an instant you worry about her being hit but bury the thought and keep going.

But she's still running after you down the street and her high heels are clacking against the sidewalk. You're losing your breath. Her heels are getting closer. She's not going to give up. You run faster. The heels are still pounding against the cement and she's still calling your name. Aw fuck it. You slow down, turn to face her. You have this sudden urge to smack her smart ass right there in the street.

Yvette comes tumbling out of breath into your arms, her chest heaving against yours. Her make-up is streaking down her face. She's holding you tight, pressing her cheeks against yours, crying, asking you what the matter is, where have you been, why do you look so bad, are you sick, she loves you, she loves you, please tell her what the matter is, please, and why did you run from her, why, why, why, why?

Now you're leaning against a store window and holding her around the waist. You hold the back of her head and try to shout at her, but your voice is too weak, and besides you're out of breath. Her eyes are wide and unbelieving.

Vaguely you are aware that a few people have stopped to watch this, that their faces are somewhere out there behind hers. You tell her that you're a dope addict. "I'm hooked on heroin," you tell her and are startled yourself at the huskiness in your voice. "I'm no good for you, you hear me? No good. Let me get myself straight and I'll he back." She doesn't believe you, she says, but you know she can tell. You push her away from you and watch her short, dark-skinned frame stand a few feet away with her hands up to her face as if she's hypnotized. She pulls on your jacket lapels. You push her away. She asks you why you did this to yourself. "They did it to me," you answer, but are lost when she asks you who they are. "Get your hands off me." You're whispering in snarls now. "I'll knock you out if you don't get your fuckin' hands off me." She bends over, crumpled, then grasps for an invisible pole. Her knees go to the sidewalk. Her neck is down so you can't see her face, only her shaking back and forth. "Don't follow me, damnit," you say, pointing at her bent head and crumpled frame on the sidewalk, and you run off into the safety of nowhere.

14

Everybody knows now. The looks are all different. It's the beginning of summer although it seems only yesterday that you left school. But it's June, not March or April anymore, and your moms has found out and almost fainted, she was so weak from hearing it.

She sits in the dark corner of your room, in the creaky chair. One arm is in her lap. She rests her right elbow on this arm. The right hand swings a handkerchief across her eyes. Her knees shake up and down. "Oh, Jesus, help me," she says. "Oh, Jesus help me. Help me...help me...please." You watch her knees jumping through the smooth apron covering her lap. She swings the handkerchief across her face. looks up to the ceiling, moans. "Why you do it to me, why? Earl, why you do it to me?" She's not even talking to you. Her voice is aimed at the ceiling, at the invisible listener she talks to so regularly. Her voice is a collection of familiar sounds: the sirens on the avenue, the squeals of children.

You've seen this before, this withdrawal, this private performance. She turns away from the world you have brought her to go elsewhere for help. Her head falls back, her knees agitate, the handkerchief crawling over her face. She begs for help and you sit there with your face feeling dull and blank and wishing you could bring some happiness to her. She moans, gasps, agitated by you, Goat. You don't know what to tell her.

What makes it so bad is how you know you look strung out but just can't get it together. You can't make the leap back to your old self. The bridge between the two selves is scary, shaky. You need the big H. And the faces in the street know you need it.

"Come on and show us something," some kids ask you as you walk past a playground. You're on your way to cop again, wearing sneaks as usual, and so saunter onto the court. You dribble, fake, fire a jumper and it's way off the mark, crashing against the backboard. Five kids look at you. You get the ball again and this time try a backward dunk. The ball grazes off the front of the rim and bounces on your head. Now you can tell they're getting impatient, and the kid who invited you is scratching his head. All right, you'll put the double dunk on them. Dribble—the ball feels good again—from the foul line and go up. You drop it through, but before you can put it through again you've lost your balance and find yourself stumbling against the metal post, your arms wide, grabbing for something to hold on to.

These are wonderful kids, you think. They should be laughing their asses off at you looking like a clumsy clown. You can't show them anything. They go back to their own game, and the kid who invited you even says thanks.

Your friends are returning from college. You can't face their questions and puzzled frowns. Dart around corners, run up the street, dash into alleys—anything to keep them from talking to you. No Rucker tournament for you. How could you play, anyway? Rudy, Bob, Bo, Dennis—you don't want to see them coming back from college and asking you how it went. You, the Goat, inventor of the double throwdown. Now you're thrown down.

You start stealing. Shit that fits in your pocket: watches, jewelry. Your habit is so big now, the little chump change you get from your moms and friends ain't hardly enough. Nobody will hire you, that's for sure, so forget about a job. You look too down-and-out. Even so, how could you report on time? You got to make it to the gallery by nine. That's always your first appointment.

You start hustling. It's easier than stealing—safer too. Your boy Van is stunned that you ask him. You are the Goat he's always looked up to, and now he looks at you the same way he looks at the other strung-out niggers. "Goat, how'd you get on this shit, man? You had so much going for you." You see he's serious, sitting in his kitty on St. Nicholas near One-Sixteen.

"Uh, I'm on it, that's the thing," you say, half laughing.

You're on the move every minute of this summer. In the morning you awake in somebody's apartment at six. Cramps. Fear. You got to start another day focused on dope. Run out, you're so desperate. Pick up the bundle of twenty-five-dollar bags and hit the streets looking for sales. By eight you hope to have sold enough to make it to the gallery. Get high. Come out at noontime still buzzing and ready to do anything. Go downtown. You're crazy enough now to rob people in broad daylight. Go into little candy stores. Catch people coming out of apartments. Stick your pistol in their backs, in their faces. You need the money. You need the dope.

At night under the whirling red lights in Harlem bars you peddle enough dope to get high yourself the next morning. You lean against doors and creep past tables. You feel like a cat rubbing its back against the furniture. The bodies in the galleries are not beings but are oversized, lumpy dolls. You walk along One Hundred-Fourteenth off Lenox in the morning after you've left the gallery and can't believe you belong to this pitiful scene. The street is filled with bodies, as if a meeting has been called. No cars can drive through. You can't walk up the sidewalk either. The entire block is stuffed with bodies like yours, no feeling, no life really, just a notion of life, of something in your memory that relates to life. Their voices are hums. They're all selling or buying and looking like death, skirting around each other, in a hurry one minute and anxiously waiting another. How did you get into this shit? You wonder as you cop a bundle or make a sale. How, Goat?

Coming down from your high, all you want to do is doze, sleep. You've definitely given up basketball for the summer. You tried to play a few games—although you had promised yourself you wouldn't—but you had no desire to win, no energy out there. The basket was so high. You were so tired. They look through you when they look at you, and you pick up your sweatshirt and get your hat.

One day you're getting off in Rush's cellar. The old hag is running around begging somebody to beat on her so a vein will pop up. The door is busted down, dust flying up your nose as the door falls and smacks flat against the dirt floor. White faces, dark blue uniforms and gold badges float through and handcuff every wrist in the place. Nobody struggles. You can't move. One of them kicks you in the stomach. You hear punches and ooh's and ah's. Soon you're marching out, leading a line of twenty of you, and you hear somebody's voice whisper loudly, "There's Earl Manigault. He used to play basketball."

You're going to prison. This is something you used to laugh at when you were a kid. Going to prison. Ha, that's funny, that's for those hoodlums. Now you're on your way, you tell yourself as you sit in the police van and face a line of addicts sitting on the bench across from you.

Use and possession. Fifteen hundred dollars or four days. Call your moms or do four. Hell, you can't call her—no way. You'll lay in the Tombs, hell. They fingerprint you, flash photo bulbs in your face, advise you of your rights, push you around like you're nobody, take your clothes and clang the metal door shut in your face. You've never seen a door key that large.

Free, you look hungrily for a fix. "Whatsa matter, Earl, you sick? You look like a ghost," says some woman who you guess hasn't heard the story.

You tell her that you are. Three blocks from this conversation is tape city, One-Hundred Eighteenth, where everybody is taped up and where anybody can cop at any time. On the corner of St. Nicholas you see a woman about your mother's age drugged deep into tomorrow. Her eyes are almost shut as she nods and staggers, selling nickel bags while two children—they must be hers—stand by clinging to her skirt. Bingo, Blue Star, Dynamite, Dick Down—you name it, they got it.

You see Betty, a bitch you've known since high school. She's overweight now, sloppy, looking like a movie monster with her crossed-eyes. The loose soles of her shoes flap against the sidewalk as she moves through and around the bodies of addicts cluttering the sidewalk and the street. You ask her to let you hold something until you can score again. You just got busted in Rush's. Yeah, she heard about it.

"You got a place to crib? You were staying with Herman, weren't you?" she asks, her mouth working as if she is chewing gum. Bodies bump into yours. Bingo, Blue Star, Dynamite, Dick Down.

"Naw, I ain't got a place." You scratch the scruff on your cheek. You smile to yourself. No way in the world you'd go back and let your moms see you. But you're so fucked-up you haven't even thought of where you will sleep. She gives you two bags and points toward Eighth Avenue. Just go to the third floor, she tells you, placing the key in your hand.

You fly up the street faster than you went to the candy store as a kid. You see nothing of the noses and ears you pass. Up the steps, three at a time. Inside, a crew of roaches is crawling over the needles and soda caps and teaspoons on the bathroom sink. Ignore the odor of an unmade bed and dirty underwear. You get the works together in no time, then go into the living room and sit on one of the wooden crates. It's late afternoon and you can hear the dribbling of basketballs in Morningside Park. This time you stick the needle in the big vein in your left arm. You wonder who's out there playing. The walls swing around your head in a circle. The ball is bouncing, then there are two balls bouncing and then the balls are rumbling against the backboard. The squeals of little kids and sirens move away from your mind as if they are on the wings of a pigeon.

You think you'll smoke a cigarette before you go off completely. Walk over to the mattress against the wall. Light up. Lie down. Wonder how your son is doing. You sure don't want him on this shit. Wonder what kind of ball Alcindor and Charlie Scott and Rudy and Bob are playing now? You know they're on a court somewhere, probably wondering about your ass. You think they have forgotten you? Naw, they wouldn't forget the Goat just like that. Cross your legs. The mattress squeaks just from that movement. You're in your sweatshirt, jeans, sneaks, ready to play ball whenever you feel you can get this bitch off your back. But not right now, oh no. The walls revolve around you, the world stops, your eyelids flutter. Here come the pink clouds ... here they come ...

Float into the beautiful reverie. You hear while floating on your back the slow dribble of Lew Alcindor. You can see him loping down the court, arms down at his side, large palms threatening. Giant mufukah, leaping and gliding through the air above everybody. Sometimes bent over mightily, hands on knees, face in somebody's face and his thoughtful eyes penetrating through. Who dunks the ball badder? Who dominates the entire court to the point where *everyone* is aware of him and must remain aware of him? You hear these kids bouncing the ball and shouting in Morningside Park and you think Alcindor is probably out there. The pink clouds coast by you as you think of Alcindor and the playground.

A sudden, deep, scratchy line is crawling up your chest, like a snake of knives. The snake burrows over your chest. It doesn't feel right at all. It's nothing like the beautiful, soft float you were just enjoying. It's an interruption, a block. This scratch—it's becoming painful—is trying to bring you down from the clouds, yet you resist.

Stay up, you tell yourself, stay up. Now there's another interruption. Voices. First the snake crawling over your chest, now voices. You resist them with all the strength you can summon, clenching your jaws, balling up your fist.

Open up in there! Open up in there! You feel the snake crawling up your chest but you won't move. *Help me break down the door.* You won't move ... voices are floating somewhere out there in the stopped world. *Look, somebody's in the bed over there...I can't see...Oh, yeah, a man,...*the snake is scratching your chest now and hands are pulling at you...*his stomach is on fire...oh, shit, look at his chest...*you hear coughing ...you see faces...fog is all over the room and you're coughing...the clouds are disappearing...the snake is still biting your chest...*pull him out of there...come on, give me a hand ... hey buddy, don't worry...*don't worry...

You can't break through the fog in your head. You know there is smoke all over the room. There are voices and there are people's shoes and bodies banging against the floor and walls. They are carrying you out of the room and screaming about a fire. Then they are taking you down the steps.

A flasher revolves on top of the ambulance. *Who is it? ...what happened? ...some dope addict burned himself up...is he dead?* You're on your back, rolling from side to side...Your chest is on fire. Your chest is on fire. Fire is part of your chest, part of you burning now so hot that you are cold.

   You look in the mirror again in the hospital dressing room. Open your shirt, the flowered shirt they gave you. Look at that shit. The purple burn mark looks like sausage links glued to your chest. Gotdamn, Goat. You button your shirt again. Scratch your cheek. You are seized with a coughing spell. This is some ugly shit. Burned your fucking chest and didn't even realize it. Plus the doctor said you contracted pneumonia. The whole damn room is burning up and you're spaced out on the mattress, flames crawling over you. What excuse can there possibly be for this? Next time you'll kill yourself.

   Leave Metropolitan Hospital and be glad that you're on East Side. Five blocks over and your moms would know about this shit. You are a sad case. You know it, too. But what can you do? You'd like to stop somebody on the street and ask, what can I do? Just help me, please. How much lower can you go? Where is the end of this?

   Now you got to hustle your ass off to pay back Betty for the damage done to her room. Your chest is so tender you can barely stand the touch of a shirt lying against it, so don't even talk about somebody bumping into you.

   By the end of the summer you can touch it without the pain overwhelming you. You run into Romeo in a corner bar, learn his smart lawyer has gotten him out with just five months. He's amazed to find that you're mainlining now, although the word is all over Harlem. He's one of the few dudes you don't turn your head from. You've been darting, sliding, sneaking around corners, into hallways, up alleys to keep from facing the astonished looks on the faces of your friends. That's why you don't want to see Yvette. You can't hurt her any more. She gave up going to school for your ass, and look at you.

   You're reminded again of the whole school thing when you see Romeo. Both of you are scratching your backs against the walls of a dark corner as you look for a hustle in the bar. You both were supposed to be out there, doing it to death, kicking ass—he as a fashion designer, you as the baddest thing next to Lew Alcindor, and some would say you are badder than Lew. Although you can't find the strength to get away from it, you still know what your life should have been like before the big H grabbed at you and snatched you off your feet. You both are going down together.

So you hook up with Romeo and you get an apartment downtown, close to your moms. Months leap by, and before you know it a year has passed and it's just as cold in Manhattan as it was when you arrived from Charlotte. You're hustling your ass off and stealing too. Arrested twice for narcotics possession, but Romeo and his attorney bail you out. You take one store for fourteen hundred dollars in cash and buy enough dope for a week. Plus, buy some clothes, treat all your addict friends to some smack and drink when they drop by the crib. You're still afraid every time you must go out there, but you go out anyway with another thirty-two caliber you had to buy after you were busted in the shooting gallery.

Another summer arrives. You haven't played basketball in over a year. You hate to walk past the playground. One Saturday you get a ball and dribble around a small court way up in the Bronx, where nobody can see you. You look for the old feel. You miss your first shots. But after you get warmed up, you start popping from all over. Soon you are lost in the effort to reclaim a portion of what you once had. You're out of breath, and the sudden workout after a layoff of all these months has you half-dead from exhaustion. You head fake, drive, twist in a lay-up. Throw the ball against the backboard, catch it at the foul circle and slam it in. Then you have enough confidence to try the backward dunk. Don't hesitate, go—you tell yourself as you stand at the foul line. You drive, lift, strain for the air and feel suddenly that your body is heavier than it's ever been because you can feel the effort it's taking to get your feet off the ground. This is taking more of your strength than anything you've done in a year. You're punishing yourself—for what, you can't say. Something inside is pushing you, brought you out here in the first place. You glide in the air and then twist in a circle so the sky spins around your head and then your fingers throw the ball backward. It goes through. You bend over, facing the foul line, then sit on the ground. Your shoulders jump up and down. You can't get enough air through your nostrils and you sit there breathing deeply, your face wet, your legs aching. Then you look up for the voices.

Three kids—they look like eleven or twelve—are standing outside the court staring at you. Their faces tell it all. They are stunned at the performance you've given. You look back at them. They turn to each other, poke each other, giggle, then come over to where you are sitting and stand around you. Finally one speaks, his voice high like a girl's, stuttering, looking at your sneaks, not in your face.

"Are you Oscar Robertson, mister?"

You snicker. Then the other two snicker and start punching the kid who just spoke. "Naw, I'm nobody," you say, rising. "Here, you want this?" Give him the ball for making your day. They dribble around, shouting as you leave the court.

You hear about the Rucker Tournament this summer. Pablo Robinson's razzle-dazzle is supposed to be hell. Freddie Crawford, Willis Reed, Nate Bowman, Archie Clark are the names you hear of the pros. Connie Hawkins from Brooklyn. Johnny Green, Bobby Hunter, Ron Jackson, Luther Green. You know them all, seen them play. Still, the only way you'll watch them is by sitting in Bob's or Mark's or Dennis' car. He'll stop, pull over to the side while you ride shotgun and you'll watch, nodding at a hip move or play, itching to get out there yourself.

"Hey, come on out and show us something," one player says as he walks up to the car from behind. He's serious. They're still some people in your corner, you see, still some people who'd like to see you get your shit together. You smile, dazed, your eyes so red he must know you're high, and that's all you can do is smile and shake your head, a silent way of telling him that you can't show him or anybody else anything. Not yet, you keep telling yourself —not yet.

But when, Goat? If you could just make that initial step, you'd be on your way to recovery. Just the beginning. That's all you need.

Days later, your head bobbing as your ass adjusts itself on a cement stoop, you hear and feel the presence of two kids. One of their hands is going into your pants pockets. It's One Hundred- Fifteenth, where addicts fill the streets and stoops and hallways. You want to jump up and snatch one of the kids, but the clouds bouncing off your forehead knock you back into your stupor. Just that one step would put you back on the right track. But minutes later you discover as the arms are shaking your shoulders that the kids are not robbing you. They have taken money off you to buy you a fish sandwich, and now they're trying to get you to eat it.

The summer speeds by. You can't even remember if the New York Stars beat out Sweet & Sour or if the Courtsmen won the Rucker Tournament. School time approaches with the dying of the leaves. Book bags and pencil sharpeners fill up the candy stores. It's chilly at night. Now addicts stop you to ask you what you got. Police cruisers crawl up to you and patrolmen ask if you're staying clean—their way of telling you they're watching you, so be careful. You've seen them rough-up women and old men, pushing their shiny black styleless shoes into these niggers' asses.

They detest you and want you to know you'll never get much rest as long as you're on the other side of the law.

One night you and Romeo are awakened by them. You share the bedroom, two mattresses on the floor. At your forehead is a gun startling you as your eyelids push through the heavy sleep. Look over to Romeo's bed. The other cop has his white hairy hand around Romeo's neck with a pistol lip against Romeo's temple. They have broken through the door. The man downstairs has complained of noise, they explain. You know it's bullshit. What noise? You snoring? They will harass your asses as long as you're on the shit.

You think you're on your way or at least are closer to getting yourself straight when Mister Burns stops you on the street one day. Please don't tell me you found out I sold the luggage you gave me, you're thinking as he calls you into the store. You're embarrassed. You've known him since you were a kid and he has to see your drooping face. He's moving around the counter and talking without looking at you, talking about these new street academies sponsored by big companies downtown—Chase Manhattan, Celanese, IBM, he can't remember them all. They're for high school dropouts who want an education. His friend, Livingston Wingate over at the Urban League told him. The Urban League's running it. They need counselors to give help and to talk to young kids in the neighborhood. Well, think about it.

You do know something about it. Used to drop in on the academy across from Colonial Park. All the young dudes now in junior high and high school sit around and rap. Claim they're wasting their time going to school. You never did understand the whole thing. Some corporations downtown are paying the Urban League to open these storefronts so dudes and sisters who don't want to go to school can tip to the storefronts and lay dead for the day. What kind of sense does that make?

"You don't understand that shit?" asks Motorman. "You don't understand that money is nothing to the big-time man downtown. All he want is publicity. He ain't looking to educate black folks. If he was he'd send some of *his* people up to Harlem to teach. All he wanna do is write a check and wipe his conscience clear. No involvement, no contact. No sympathy for us. And that jive Urban League, all they do is funnel the money from the man to the niggers. Somebody black *got* to do it, Goat, so it gotta be either the Urban League or the NAACP. Who else, can Chuck trust? You or me ain't *never* gonna get money from no big corporation or foundation, and we know more people in Harlem than the law allows."

Sit half-dazed in the park and nod, agreeing with everything Motorman says. The nigger always did have some smarts. Maybe he know what he talkin' about. You know everytime you stop in on the academy here or at the downtown, niggers be sitting around rapping. You saw one dude nodding and talking about what college he wanted to attend. Nigger spaced out on horse and honestly sitting there with his arms folded and talking about going to college. But Motorman makes some sense. They didn't care about you when you was in school. They don't care about any of us. Shuffle through, that's all. You can't read or write or do nothing and you get promoted to the next grade where you still don't learn anything. Push them in, push them out. Next class, please. Ah, more dumb niggers here to play sports and smoke dope and talk shit to the white girls and raise hell with switchblades.

"Their kids getting educated, aren't they?" asks Motorman. "They don't have street academies in Scarsdale or Upper Montclair or Greenwich, do they, Goat? Their kids go to Princeton and Amherst after high school."

To hear Motorman tell it, it's just one big ripoff. Money goes through people's hands and they look good. But nobody gets educated, hardly. It sounds good. It looks good. But it ain't good. It gets some niggers an opportunity to sit down and rap together. Gets some niggers some jobs. Pulls some niggers off the street. But you watch—and Motorman digs his finger in your chest—ten years from now the school system be more fucked-up than it is now and nobody be going to school or getting educated. You'll have to go to private school to get educated. And how many niggers can afford that?

But Skip sits on the bench and runs down another line when the subject turns to the academies. He says that we gotta start somewhere, that the companies do mean good, that people are learning in the academies, that it isn't a ripoff. Motorman erupts, jumps off the bench in the park, turns in a circle, stamps his feet and disagrees. Others on the bench, including yourself, laugh. Skip says, "Aw man," and waves Motorman away with a hand thrown in Motorman's direction. But Skip looks flustered; his light-skinned face has turned a deep shade. "Aw man," he says.

"Aw man, hell," says Motorman. You all laugh with him. He's chumped Skip into silence. Your boys get up from the bench and look up into the sky and ignore Skip.

Go to the Urban League office. All the chairs in the waiting room are filled with dudes you know. Fluorescent lights, typewriters clicking, muddled voices. A lady takes your name, asks you questions, then looks at you strangely when you can't answer half of them. "You've *never* had a job before?" she asks, her head tilted down to the paper she's writing on.

Don't know how, but you get the job and keep it for a month until they are tired of your reporting to your academy late. Two out of three days you're late, the other times you don't even show. You never even see any of the kids you're supposed to counsel. By the time you make it to the academy, they've gone on a field trip or got tired of waiting for you.

You're high when they fire you. "What'd I do?" you ask. You're crazy enough to say anything, they'd better watch it. Here you are with your hands on the counter, your head rocking back and forth, knowing you ain't worked ten days in the last month and supposed to be helping kids who hang out in the streets and shoot up just like you. And you want to know what you did.

"You haven't done anything," says the plump, yellow woman, the administrative director, fanning the pages of a report in your face. "That's why you're fired. You don't have the discipline to encourage young men to discipline themselves. Please leave." She looks you right in the eye. You hear soles scraping across the floor behind you. She's serious. A shadow of a man's figure turned sideways is waiting, looking, behind her. You suck your teeth, turn, glance at the people sitting in chairs lining the walls of the reception area, tip out. It's hard to be big, feel big when you're constantly running into jolting reminders that you're nothing. Mister Burns will bear about this, too—shit.

All they know is doing shit the way the white man taught them. You can't always run shit in the ghetto like that. We don't understand all that shit about timetables and precision and planning. You did your job. You helped more kids stay off dope than Carter has liver pills. All right, sure, you didn't get to the gig on time always. But you got there. You love kids. Wouldn't do nothing to hurt a kid. You talked to them—more than what their parents do. You gave them advice. Showed them some moves. Now this bitch gonna talk shit about you didn't get there on time. Fuck you, Sapphire. Take the Goddamn job and ...

Fall passes you by and then it's cold again, and then it's spring. You're a big-time pusher and user now. Hey, hey, hey, people speak to you still. You hear somebody say something about 1969. He can't mean this year, you think. Jump into a cab and run down to One-Fourteenth.

Kids dribble balls along the sidewalks and you watch them with your cheek resting against your palm. Seems as if all the same kids are playing in the same streets whenever you ride down Amsterdam. How nice it would be to start over again, be a kid like these kids with your life not yet worked out, the possibilities still there. Not like you are now, a pair of hand-me-down sneaks just about, kicked over to the side of the locker room and people coming by to glance at you and stare away. You wish you weren't even in your own skin, wish you didn't have to do half the things you must do. If you were like those kids out there you wouldn't have to be doing this shit, Goat. Life slips away so quickly and before you know it, you can't do too much about it. One year is two years is three years.

And all those dudes who will be playing in the Rucker this summer are the cats you grew up with. Some of them in college and doing what they supposed to be doing. Some in high school and going on to college. You consider how you should be moving ahead too, going higher than them as if you're going up for a rebound, but the shit didn't break and you find pain instead of what should have been. Everybody is moving ahead, seems like, Rudy, Bob, Motorman. Pablo with the Globetrotters. Jimmy Walker from Providence College, he'll be in the Rucker—brothers and sisters laying for him already. You talking about the pros now, the real kings and princes of ball in the nation and playing right here. Pablo could trick an auditorium. Freddie Crawford and Bob McCullough can fire the Pill, make no mistake. Little Frankie, Frankie Townsend, you saw him the other day, he playing. Big Willis Reed, give him position and your shit is over, the way he muscles in. Of course the Hawk from Brooklyn, most definitely the baddest because he can fly, swoop, do something that will get you to scratch your head. Damn, Goat, you know all these brothers, used to run with them and show *them* shit. They'll be running this summer, and you—temporarily on leave from the world because of circumstances beyond your control. You hooked on the Big H, the horse, the bitch, the lady who knows no discrimination, who takes anybody at anytime. Shit, what she care about whose life she ruining, just ruin a motherfucking life, that's all. Happens to be yours—tough, tough shit. Pass on please.

It's almost eleven-thirty anyway. Your source will have left five bundles in the hallway. Jump out of the cab into the din. The walking dead crowd the block. You're desperate. again, need the bread to cop for yourself and think about getting your shit together. You don't see anybody and see everybody.

Walk fast, heart patters. Pains zip through your stomach. You hate yourself but can't stop what drives you, not now anyway.

Marvin Gaye is in your head. *Poor, simple-minded. You'll go crazy.* You're bent over at the shoulders, can feel them weighing down your body. *You go to the place where danger awaits you.* Eyes getting fuzzy again. Heart zips. Breathing through your mouth. *Poor, simple-minded. The place where danger awaits you.* A chorus of warnings flow through you, but you can only say yes, you hear them, and then press forward. Stumble in a dark, warm haze as if entering the steps of a castle, looking like the White House, big dome, very white, haze lurking around it and the chorus greeting you. *The place where danger awaits you.* Go on. Hurry, now, hurry.

There he is, same dude with the big ears you been selling to for months. Foggy haze disappears. Little cap. Belted raincoat, hands in pocket. Give him the signal, go into the hallway. There's the package on the floor. He pushes open the door and enters. A baby cries upstairs. Mother yells at it to shut up. He has all the telltale signs in his eyes and cheeks. He's on it heavy. Five bundles, one hundred and twenty-five dollars each. That's two-fifty twice making five hundred plus another buck and a quarter makes six hundred and twenty-five dollars. He's been buying three bundles a day, spending three seventy-five. Today he's going big, wants five bundles. Shit, this is like getting a raise.

"Gettin' warm again, huh Goat?" He's checking the bundles.

"Why you checking now, you think I'd cheat you after all this time?" Your fists are at your sides, you're half dazed, the money's in your pocket, you're doing good.

"Cause the shit will have to stand up in court." He straightens up, pulls out a badge with one hand and a pistol in another. "You're under arrest."

You can't do a thing but sigh deeply. "Why'd you wait so long if you the police?"

He ushers you out of the hallway, into the street and around the corner where his partner waits in an ugly, dented blue car. You're handcuffed. The world goes by, continues although yours is stopped. They're both talking to you but you're elsewhere, not here. Looking out the window means nothing as objects pass by from left to right. This dude's been buying from you for months and suddenly he's a cop. He's got to be hooked, otherwise why'd he take so long? Ain't that a bitch. An addict on the police force. Who's going to believe you?

Bite your nails. Jive nigger's talking to you but you hear no words, know only the sound of a voice in the car. What scares you more than anything is that you haven't copped. You'll be shivering and nodding tonight. Streaky lines of pain will dart through your stomach; sweat will rinse your face. They'll probably keep your ass until tomorrow. Criminal. That's what they'll be calling you now. Think of all the shit and people you've ripped off in the last year—or was it two years? Hundreds of thousands of dollars to support your life on the big H. Four, five hundred dollars a week. That's what it takes.

Bite your nails, look out the window with your neck now going limp as your head bobs. They've taken the Westside Highway and it looks something like Seventy-Ninth Street and you see in your head that first day you are in the garment district. A Friday. Jump out the car in a light drizzle of rain and pull on the tip of your sky. It's a white cap you bought downtown. Run to the other side of the street, your sneaks slapping against the street. Spit on the sidewalk, take a deep breath, check out the parade of handcarts and hand trucks being pushed by the brothers and Puerto Ricans. Your eyes are on the dolly of fur coats in a king it down the avenue. Six fur coats swing on hangers. Two police stand on the diagonal corner. Dart across Seventh Avenue again—a car whizzes by your ass—and walk up quickly to the line of doilies. Get behind the dude who's got his back bent into pushing his dolly. The police twirl their sticks on the corner. Trucks rumble down the street. "Hey," you shout, knowing this is wild and crazy and dangerous, but so is your life and the need to continue. The dude pushing the platform of fur coats turns his head around without stopping.

"Hey, wha's happnin'?"

Walk up to his side. The light has changed and stopped him at the corner. One dolly has just gotten across the street. New Yorkers are buying hot pretzels, franks and orange sodas from a stand under the light. Light drizzle is like a mist. Go into your pocket. "I want one of them coats." Just like Romeo told you. Act like you know exactly what you're doing. The dude's eyes go blank as if he has heard the most disappointing news in the world. It occurs to you that it's about April, same time of year as now. Stick your gun into his back. "Whatcha gonna do, man?" He tells you to take it. The light changes, you walk past him, take a coat off the rack in the April morning of downtown Manhattan with two cops on the corner. Leave the hanger, throw the coat over your arm, reverse your direction and walk down the sidewalk. Stop a block away, unfold the paper bag which is in your jacket pocket and drop the coat into the bag. Head toward Eighth

Avenue and an uptown-bound cab to Harlem where you will sell the shit for enough dope to keep you going for awhile. Then you go to get off in somebody's cellar and start thinking about the next day and the next week.

Better than the garment district—you consider as you shift position in the police car and half-hear the jive motherfucker talking right at your ear about how he saw you play one day— are the times you went into the East Side. You tell the driver, "Madison and Sixty-Ninth." These are the people who own it all, prance about with their poodles and cashmeres and minks. The streets are cleaner, the shops sell shit you can't even find in Harlem. You don't see all the garbage either. It's dusk and the sky is colored orange. A man eases backward out of a long, black Continental, out of the back seat as if he is pulling a package from the floor. His left hand sparkles—two giant stones. Meanwhile, the doorman is in the street and waving down a cab for an old lady covered with black: hat, coat, shoes, bag. As the man goes into the building under the canopy which reads, "Regency," you follow. His feet clatter down the marble hallway toward the elevator. Sweat spreads over your face. It's later summer of last year. He is Chinese. Wait casually for the elevator. The doors rumble open. He pushes '12', then you push '10'. Look down like the obedient delivery boy you're supposed to be. Doors open, you get off. The floor is carpeted. Dart down the hallway to find the stairway. You see EXIT on the right, push open the door, run up the steps in great leaps, hopes, praying the muthafukah hasn't gotten off and made it to his apartment, hustle up the next landing of six steps, pull the door open with a great rush of air following, peer down the hall to see the elevator numbers light up. Leap down the hallway to the elevator, slam your back and hands against the wall and wait. Catch the Chinese man just as the shiny black shoe steps from the elevator. Spin him around by the shoulder and point the .32 caliber at him.

"Give me the rings—take them off your hand." His lips tremble, eyes about to cry. Where is all the power and arrogance now? The rings slide off, clink into your hand. "Let me have your wallet. No I'll get it," shaking it with one hand. A five and two ones float out. What? He only has seven dollars to his name? You lean to pick up the bills, then back into the elevator. Your forehead and wrists sweat. The doors come together. Lean, spent, against a wall of the elevator. Chest rises and falls. How long have you been in the elevator? You haven't pushed the button. Imagine that shit— two diamonds worth maybe a grand, and seven dollars in cash. Cheap bastard.

And now off the Westside Highway and down to Canal where the trucks rumble along the cobble street and sway almost into the car you're riding in. And the detective's voice, the jive fukah who's been getting high with you since last winter, is still droning in that monotone as the scene of your ripping off that Chinese dude dissolves. Right turn at Centre Street.

You're at the Tombs. New York City Detention Penitentiary. Possession of a dangerous narcotic. Sale of a dangerous drug. Multiple offender. Previous arrest record. Bail is fifteen hundred. Court appearance. Warnings and suggestions, statistics and figures fly past your mind. Can't contact your attorney. Who else? Name of nearest relative. That means your moms. She's going to find out.

Her mouth is wide open when she sees you an hour later. Two gray hairs arch through her hair net. She's in her best wear—gloves, long black coat with the fur collar, white scarf. "You been on this dope for three years," she says. You're amazed. It was just yesterday that you came home from school. But she says it's 1969. You can't talk to her, can hardly look at her sitting on the other side of the table. "Why do you do this to me?" she asks. You start crying. She pushes her hand through the wire and grabs you by the neck, begins to squeeze, then pulls back and turns her head away from you. Now she's crying. She's whining, her voice choking and rising and stuttering about how much she loves you and how could you do this to yourself. You out there with hoodlums, robbing and stealing and killing yourself, like common ordinary hoodlums. Why you turn so rotten? Why, why? You can't even think about answering.

She takes you home in a cab. You know she's going to scold you. She tells you she wants you to move back to the hotel and leave that Romeo alone. She wants you to be a man. Are you going to be just like your father? Are you going to roll in the gutter until you kill yourself? Don't you ever think about others? Have you no decency, no self respect? Don't you know all white people think we're animals anyway, and you're acting just like one? How can you live with yourself? Don't you care at all about her, your mother? Who else you got when she go? She loves you like nobody. But you must get out that gutter.

At the hotel, you go into your room and throw your body down on the mattress. Look into blackness as you lie on your back. Yvette, your moms, Rucker, your son—you've let every-body down. You are dust that should be swept up and dumped. You ought to throw yourself into a trash can.

You're scared as you lie on this mattress. As much as your mother has been hurt by you, as much as so many people have been hurt by you,

you are afraid that you still can't stop. Maybe you can hold off for a few days but you just ain't ready, you don't have the strength yet to make a clean break. It'll come. It'll come, but it ain't in you yet. Your hands shake. You're scared. You know you will have to do it. You know you have to go back out. To the place where danger awaits you. *Stupid minded* ...

15

Days later you see some of the fellows on the bench in Colonial Park. You flying high now on this hot day in August. Heart is beating fast, sun is beating down on you, your steps are springy. Bob, Fred, Julio, Mark and others sit on the bench. Nods, handshakes. You squeeze out a seat. Conversation picks up. Smile, not knowing exactly where you are except your knees are knocking against the legs of your boys sitting on either side of you. Nod in agreement at everything they say although you aren't sure what it is they are saying. Big Lew getting over a million from the Bucks. Over a million dollars. How much dope could that buy? What could you do with a million dollars? The Hawk going to the Phoenix Suns after all the bullshit they ran him through. Home boys doing good in the big time. Everybody talks about Lew and Hawk as if they know them personally. The pros. Seems like a dream out there now, something you had a chance at before it slipped away. Only half here. Your high pulls you elsewhere. Sit on this bench and listen to the stories of cats making it now. Sit drugged and spaced and smiling. Then the talk shifts to Kenny Bellinger. Young brother destined for success. Sure bet for full ride in college and no question about the pros. Terrorizes young boys throughout the city. You nodding yep, yep, yep—half here anyway, don't really know the brother that well. You've seen him move—definitely has speed and a good shot. You nodding yep, yep, he's a bad dude all right, when suddenly the sentences begin to slap you in the face. You keep hearing them talk about tragedy and falling and dope addiction until finally you aren't smiling anymore. You sit up and focus your tired eyes on the sky.

You aren't smiling because they're talking about how Bellinger was on the shit and ripped off this old lady by climbing down to her bedroom window by a fire escape. How he must have needed the shit real bad to be doing something crazy like that. How he was only 16. "Hadn't even had the crabs yet," says Bob. A kid. What happened? You wonder, but can't ask because you're supposed to be *listening,* Goat. You are there with them, aren't you? Lady screams and calls the cops. Bellinger jumps out the window, crawls up the 'scape to the roof, runs across the roof. Cops chase after him, said they fired in the air. Bellinger tries to jump across to another roof—ain't nowhere else to go—and never even gets close to the other side. He falls from this rooftop and splatters on the sidewalk on Eleventh.

Your stomach muscles jump. "That shit will make you do all kinds of crazy shit," says one of the voices. "Young boy, had the world in his fingertips and blew it for some smack. Can you imagine that shit? Who could be so stupid as that—to fuck up a life over some useless shit like dope. Imagine that, man—giving your life to some motherfucking powdered shit to stick in your muthafuckin' bloodstream just to feel good. You know that shit is crazy." Agreements, nods, agreements, nods. Dazed. Your stomach is still jumping. Young boy on dope runs from cops and falls from rooftop.

Time for you to tip. Shit is getting depressing and personal. Slide off the bench, start toward the sidewalk, turn to give them a fist goodbye. Over to Forty-Fifth and St. Nicholas. Think about Kenny Bellinger jumping between buildings. You can see his body, hurtling through the air with the chimneys and antennas in the background. Hurtling and falling to the sidewalk. Scary shit, Goat. Scary.

Jump into a cab, direct the driver to the Eighties. Sidewalks filled with niggers as you shoot down St. Nicholas: music, screams, laughs, hand clasps, dance steps, basketball moves, boxing contests—the rhythm of the ghetto. But you are frightened now. That young boy's body splattered on the sidewalk sticks in your mind. You want to see Yvette and Darrin right now so you'll know you have somebody. These brothers and sisters out here don't care about you. But Yvette does, you can believe that. You are scared now and need somebody. Kenny Bellinger dead at 16. Googobs of talent.

Bloodstream still excited, you wrestle yourself out of the cab and hustle up Broadway where the bright, hazy sun blinds you more and the walkers up the sidewalks are so many obstacles. You stop a moment to watch a Puerto Rican cab driver shout at another driver in Spanish. They're in the middle of Eightieth Street. The other driver's front fender has dented the cab's side. Police siren and flashing light break from your right. Buses and trucks snarl and hiss. Pedestrians bump into each other. The Puerto Rican cab driver is raising his arms in screams while the other driver sits in his car and wipes his forehead with his arm. Turn off toward West End. A white girl and a black girl play hopscotch. You see the high-rises in New Jersey, the sky is that clear. Now between West End and Riverside you slow down and, missing a step, almost stumble into the entrance of the apartment building. The buzzer lets you in.

When you get off the elevator on the third floor you turn to see Yvette standing in the doorway down the hall. Big, big smile. She comes out. Now down the hall. She hugs you.

"Hey, easy on the neck."

"I had the funniest feeling you would come by today." She's ahead of you and dragging your arm down the hall.

"You just in time for lunch. Hungry?"

"Naw, I ate. What is it?"

"Leftover spaghetti and meatballs. Better than yesterday when I cooked it."

"Where's Darrin?"

"Darlene took him to Coney Island. He gettin' big, Earl."

"Yep." Sit on the plastic-covered couch in the living room. "How long's it been?"

"Months, Earl."

She stands in front of you. You can see her pretty well except for the slight tinge of a blur bouncing in front of you. Her eyes, the tilted head, the cheeks—they're the same. You wouldn't come by during the spring or winter. You felt too bad. Too much like a criminal. You have your pride. You're high now, but at least know what you're doing. Hold out your hands. "Come on and sit down by me." Your voice is like a whisper; one reason you hate for her to see you.

"Did you know about Kenny Bellinger?" Her head lies on your shoulder as you both look across the room at two chairs and some plants. Her hands are folded into yours. She nods yes. You stare at the wall as she eases her fingers over your hands. "What possessed him to try some shit like that? That shit was crazy. Trying to jump between buildings, and at night, too. It scared me, Yvette."

She gets up to check the spaghetti, and her thin, flowery robe swishes past you. "Be right back," she says. Her bowl of spaghetti is steaming when she returns. She puts a forkful up to your lips. You have no appetite. You swallow. As soon as it hits your stomach it starts back up like a lump. You try to make it to the doorway of the bathroom. Stomach still jumping, you look around for the mop, but Yvette pushes you back toward the couch.

Hands in your pockets, you pace behind her as Yvette kneels to clean up your mess. You think she's crying because she's taking so much time down there and not talking either. Sit back down.

"I gotta do something about this." Almost like talking to yourself, but you know she knows it's to her. Still staring ahead. Her fork clinks in the bowl. Then she's finished and going back to the kitchen and now standing in front of you with her flowery cotton robe, buttons up the middle.

"What do you want to do, Earl?"

"I ... I . . ." Look with confusion at her belly. What is it you want? "I want to come back ... to life. I'm dead now, Yvette. I'm not even here now, you know. I want to get off this shit. I wanna be normal. Next thing you know, I'll be falling off a rooftop."

"You can do it. I'll help you. You can do it, Earl. Really."

The opening between two buttons shows perfectly the few smooth strands of hair on her belly. Press the side of your face against the warm belly. Your hands wrap around her waist. She rubs her long fingers along the backs of your ears and then over to your shoulders. Trucks rumble along the street to your right. Your hands go down her back, to the soft but firm pillows. No elastic line of panties, just the smooth, soft lines of Yvette. Her thighs. You squeeze them and go on to the back of the knees, and even lower, to her ankles where the little bones stick out. Now you face her and put your forehead and nose against her flowery robe, slip your tongue inside the crack of space. She shivers when your tongue lifts the hairs on her stomach. More trucks rumble by. Yvette's fingers massage your cheeks and the back of your neck. One finger goes across your eyelids. Drawing lines over your face. You're supposed to do something, but aren't sure if you can. But her fingers ease across your upper lip, tickle your lips which twitch. Hold her wrists. Kiss her palms and fingers. Press your face into her palm's and kiss the little lines going every which way. And then you want to kiss her wrists, tease the tiny hairs on her wrists. Now while you are kissing her hands, her beautiful, tan palms with the funny, dark lines, she pulls away. She takes your hands now and invites you to rise from the couch, and before anything registers in your mind she is leading you toward the bedroom.

The sun is everywhere, blinding you. It blasts through the sheer curtains and flings its light over the walls, the dresser, the bedspread. You blink. Yvette pulls down the shades, and standing in the doorway, you watch without squinting now that the room is darker. In three movements—a bent elbow, a bend at the waist, a turn—she is beautifully and suddenly naked, and with the same speed has glided under the spread and lies waiting for you.

"Hurry."

You stumble. Your laces get stuck. But in seconds you are in the bed with your woman on a hot, sunny afternoon. The little boy, your son, is away. Yvette's parents are away. You are tired, confused, half-blurred in another world. You cuddle yourself into this woman who you know will do anything for you at any time, who loves you, who lives for you. How could you have done what you've done to yourself, knowing at the same time you've hurt her? She moans, kisses your eyelids, your cheeks, your nose. Her arms squeeze so tightly around your neck. She moans, squeezes you while you nestle your body into the warmth and softness that is her body. And that is all you can do—nestle, cuddle, settle yourself into her body. That's all you can do.

"What's the matter?" It's a whisper. But also a cry. You sense panic, fear.

"I don't feel it, that's all." Your voice is so raspy, it sounds to you like another person's speaking. "I don't feel it."

All the tightness, the tension, the energy—all the feeling you sensed from her moments earlier have turned limp now. Her body isn't the same now—it's loose, droopy, so much softer. Great portions of feeling have dribbled away from her.

"I don't feel it, Yvette. I gotta get off this shit for real now." She's crying. Loud. Try to muffle her voice with kisses, but she turns her face back and forth and cries loudly. They're moans, really, reminding you of Mommagran's low, throaty singing from the kitchen when you were a child. Her stomach lifts and falls under you. Her nose is wet. Shoulders shake and shake you. The moans are coming from your memory, from a past scene breaking through to you here today. You're trying to hold down something rising from your stomach, but every cry of hers pulls it farther until the burning rises from your chest to your throat and you too, Goat, are crying. Cry with her, hold her, your shoulders shaking too. So your nose gets too stuffy and your face is wet and hot and your eyes are burning until everything goes ...

Both of you awaken to find yourselves staring into each other's eyes. You sit up on the side of the bed. Drowsy still. Yvette's hand rubs your shoulders and moves over your chest and suddenly jerks away as it touches the burn marks. Although her hand settles back on your chest it's too late now. You know how ugly the burn looks and feels. Somebody must have planned this day for you. First you learn about Kenny Bellinger, then you don't have enough in you to make love to your woman, then the scars from the burn you got while being doped-up scare her. How much more do you need? Walk over to the mirror. Where's the muscle and toughness that used to be in your body? The eyes dull, reddish. Your hair nappy, growing every which-away. Cheeks sagging. What happened to the Goat, inventor of the double dunk, scored 52 against Watley? What happened? Sigh, sit back down on the bed. Get back under the covers.

Yvette's now in front of the mirror and picking her hair with that fast motion of hers. "What do you want to do, Earl?"

"Get off it. Get off the shit. I can't keep it up."

"How do you get off it?"

"You can stop, that's all. But nobody stops. Nobody beats the horse. She gets your ass and keeps it forever. Kenny Bellinger couldn't stop. He was robbing and stealing every day just like me, and probably hating it just like me, but he couldn't stop. I don't know how you do it." Turn sideways in the bed, your face on the pillow. She's in her robe now at the doorway.

"You have to stop, then. Just like that."

She says nothing. You expect her to go on, but there's silence. Another minute it seems, and still silence. Lift your head to look at her. Her eyes burn back. At the doorway she stands, serious as all get out. The frown on her forehead is serious.

"Okay, I'll just stop like that. Simple as that. Solid, I stopped just now." You hate the raspiness in your voice.

"Go to the Tombs and stay there until it's all out of your system. If you're serious, you can do it. That's it, Earl."

The words jolt your insides. She's talking about a serious cold turkey. Nobody does it. Cats have gone in and lasted a few days only to fall screaming on the floor and banging their heads against the walls as they cry to be released. Next day, they're out in the streets again shooting up. You don't know anybody who's done it. You don't know anybody who's beaten the lady. Is Yvette serious? Can you possibly beat it like that? You haven't seen her this serious before, ever. Now your mind projects a picture of a teenage body trying to jump across two Harlem buildings at night. Then you see yourself hating to wake up in the mornings because you know you've got to start the same shit again. Your appetite comes and goes. You don't want to fuck. You burned your gotdam chest. You gave your mother a bunch of gray hairs and tears, and now your main squeeze stands wearing the flowery robe in the doorway and tells you without question that you've got to do it.

Jumping out of the bed, you crawl into your clothes. Why even think about it? You keep telling yourself you want to change. Well, either put up or shut up. Can you put it off forever?—no. Don't think about it. Move. Now or never. Okay, now. Like coming out of the locker room at half time and behind by 20 points, you move with blank determination, knowing there are big things out there to overcome, but simply by reflex, on G.P. You have no choice but to try. Hypnotically, as if there is no alternative, you press forward. Snakes are tied. Yvette gets dressed and puts on a smile, puts music in her voice. You drink a glass of water, look out the living room window down at the waves of heat rippling along the black asphalt street. She comes up behind you, her perfume refreshing, wraps her arms around you, leads you out to the door.

Holding hands up the avenue, then a cab to your mom's. The figures of the blurry world on Ninety-Fifth begin to gel as your high falls apart. Same fags and whores and pushers holding up the lamp posts. A few dudes with basketballs, styling their new Converse sneaks and orange-striped shorts, and some kids with iced lemons pushed up to their noses. Women hang out the windows, one fixing her hair with a curling iron, another holding a baby whose bottle is about to fall out its mouth, and another, thin, has a face weak with sadness. Nods, greetings. They remind Yvette she hasn't been around for awhile. A kid swings on your arm. Through the hallway, your sneaks squeaking on the tiles and Yvette's hand in yours. Your mother stands at the end, having come out from the switchboard desk, and gives you both a gigantic smile. She hugs Yvette and then turns her head rapidly back and forth the way she does when she doesn't want to cry. Moving around the two or three tenants in the hall, you all go to your room. Yvette sits next to you on your bed and your mother sits in that favorite chair of hers and listens as you tell her that you've had it with dope. It has worn you out completely and you can't go on. You're tired of it—just tired. The lump is rising from your stomach again as you recall what it is you've been doing these last two, three years. Your moms flinches at your stories. Yvette's hand tightens. And the two of them agree to go to the prison with you as you try to beat the Iron Lady.

16

Half of them know you. You seen half of them on the streets, in the patrol cars. Blue faces move past your stare. They have clipboards, sheets of paper, belts lined with bullets. The walls are shiny, brown blocks, and the floor is shiny too. Your mother and Yvette are doing all the talking while you stand in the little office of the captain and look out through the rectangle of glass at the police station. They ask you something. You turn, nod yes. The captain is short with wide, thick arms. He probably served in the army for twenty years and then found that the police force was the closet thing to the military. All captains have a problem, you think, looking at his reflection in the glass. They want to boss people around. All police have the same problem. They're the enemy. Every cop you've seen in Harlem was bossing somebody around. Ever since you were a kid. Well, now and then they'd help an old blind lady with rheumatism across the street, but usually they going upside somebody's head or telling somebody what to do. Black ones too. They love to beat their own. It's just like the army. You the enemy and they after your ass. Whenever they can, they'll kick you, call you a jungle bunny or Sambo, spit on you, pull your arm nearly out of its socket, stick a finger in your eye, do anything to show they hate your black ass.

You turn to look and listen fully now to the three at the captain's table. Papers are twisted in the hands of the captain, are moved flat over the desk, are pushed around and read. Your moms asks questions. The captain is serious—frown ain't left his face yet. Yvette turns to look at you, smiles. You walking around like a kid whose mother is talking to the principal inside his office.

Asked to sit down, you cop a squat between your two women, the women who have always been there when you needed help. He's talking about the Rockefeller Plan, some dope rehabilitation program set up by the governor and putting your ass in jail for—how long did he say? How many years? Two? Five? But then you'd be free to start over again, like a brand new baby. No dope, no stealing and robbing after the shit is done. You'd be new. New. Your voice be back, your appetite would come back. Crawling out of the gutter is what you'd do. He's making it sound easier than it could be, you think. Yvette holds your hand. Your moms is nodding the way she does when she knows what she's doing is right. Yeah, sure, anything. Just get you off the shit. You've never been so damned disgusted. You were actually hurting yourself. Killing your own self. Naw, no more, Goat. Straighten up and fly right. Sure, any kind of plan, any kind of pain, any length of time. Just to get you off this ugly shit.

Sign the papers. Your heart patters. Everybody is looking at you, and the scratching of the pen across the paper has everyone's attention. That's how your signature looks? You never noticed. Look up to the captain staring at you. Probably figuring that you'll be here for a couple of hours before you're ready to call it quits. Remember Herman and Romeo and Black Betty and their stories. Niggers be talking shit about how they gonna get off the shit, gonna do cold turkey and come back new people. Next thing you know, they back in the cellar hungrier and needing more than they ever did before. And had the nerve to look down on you, like you didn't have the strength they had. You were nothing, everybody in the gallery was nothing. They were going to kick the shit and leave your ugly ass forever. Then they'd be back with the scariest stories of pain. Seemed as if they were trying to scare away anybody from even thinking of cold turkey. Can't be done. Can't be done, they'd say. You'd shiver. Hell, you didn't want to think of anything like that—no dope for a week. Crazy.

But now you sit back and sigh, your arms drooping down over the sides of a chair. The captain pushes a bell. Your mother's handkerchief flips in front of her face. You're standing now and Yvette is hugging you. The captain moves toward the door, opens it, and two cops come toward you. They're all waiting for you. "Let's go," you say, and then you kiss both Moms and Yvette, pull away from their arms and walk out the door.

Into the large entryway and the bustle of people. Clamor of prison sounds. *Gotta right to two phone calls. Breaking and entering. Personal recognizance. What, you back again, Charlie? Don't touch me! I said don't touch me. Keep your hands off me. Loitering. Suspicious nature. Indecent exposure.* Mostly niggers. White people must be really good. They never get locked up.

And now down the hall where a row of cells goes all the way 'til you can't see anymore. Voices scream out. Faces on either side, like puppies in a pet shop, stare at you. Your door is here, empty. Little cot, antiseptic smell, roaches crawling up the wall. Lie down and wait. It's Thursday afternoon, August and hot as hell outside, and you're in prison to kick a habit you've had for three years. You're going to wipe out all that shit in a few weeks. Sounds like one of those quiz shows where you go for the bonus and the audience is rooting for you. Just that simple, Goat, just that simple. Lie down and wait. Floating again in the familiar twilight zone. You see all these people circle around you. They're relatives—Aunt Hattie, Mommagran, your oldest brother, Benson, some friends like Mister Rucker, Romeo, Rudy. Behind them are hundreds of other people who know you. They're waving, waiting to see what you're going to do. Sit up. You thought you heard somebody call your name. Probably somebody shouting down the hall. Lie back down. Run through in your mind the routine you must accustom yourself to. Cold cereal for breakfast. Soup, potatoes, bread for lunch and dinner. Exercise an hour, where you'll mingle with the others. All this is supposed to make you a new person. All the dudes you know who been in for robbery, assault, non-support and so forth are supposed to sit in a cell and realize they did wrong, then leave as new people. How's that sound?

You'd like to be a new person. Think of all those people on the outside who ain't addicted, who lead normal, happy lives. Don't have to think twice about getting shot up before they wash their faces in the morning. Don't hate themselves for the shit they have to do. People who feel good and look good. Sure, they got their problems, but they ain't got *this* problem. This is sure enough the worst thing that could happen to anyone.

So try to think of something pleasant as you brace yourself. And it is easier to do than you think. See yourself already doing the three-sixty, your turnaround—you mean complete turn- around—against somebody in the park. Then you got the reverse three-sixty, where you throw it in backwards. The Goat. It's you up there, acrobat. You pinning the ball against the boards, old men on the sidelines almost choking on their beer. Hey, check the two-hand dunk: *bla-bloom.* Dudes talking about be cool on me today. You and Dennis and Mark and Rudy and Bob and Julio walking down the avenue with orange sodas, high in the air, all of you sporting those knee-high thick sweats, voices mingling with the mighty Temptations who blast from a greasy spoon (chops, grits and gravy, hot biscuits). Yeah, that's what you'll think about. All those pleasant grooves will sustain your ass, Goat. Don't worry.

All those pleasant grooves, yeah. But what about the reality of this shit? You think about it that evening in the dark. Of course you can't sleep the first night in jail. You scared so tough, you couldn't sleep if your life depended upon it. Resting your head on your arms folded behind your neck, check out the row of black-and-white lines against the wall, designs made by the bars of the cell lit by the ceiling bulb. And then the reality, the pain hits you in the stomach—stabs you actually, because you were just lying their thinking of some pleasant Laurinburg scene with Yvette—slashes diagonally across your stomach like a cold wire and sends you jumping. Then another wire, this one electric, stinging, slashes across from the other side of your stomach and buckles your knees. And this is only the first night? You ask yourself while you're on your knees.

It's all mind now, you tell yourself. Either your mind tells you to give up because your body can't take it, or your mind tells your body it doesn't need it, that's enough of it—go on to something else. Concentrate on you and Yvette meeting in the fields at Laurinburg. Way out there farther than the football field stretches, in the patch of low, wild grass, she twists her cotton dress in the moonlight. Despite the wires whipping across your stomach, you picture Yvette in the football field in her cotton dress. If that fades, find another. How about when you were in junior high and scored those 52 points. The other coach had asked his players, "Can't you stop him?" You remember him saying that definitely.

But then the lines curl up inside your stomach and start expanding, worm-like. So these worms jab at the lining of your stomach like hundreds of needles. Falling on all fours and thinking how you must look like one of the players searching for his contact lenses, you throw back your head and choke. Now roll on the floor—it's cold even though it's burning up inside the cell—and try to wrap yourself up with your arms. Roll onto your back and kick up your legs. You scream now as the pain changes to heavy balls banging against the sides of your stomach. You go into a sweat, shiver, bang your body backward into the corner. Hold it, hold it, Goat. Inventor of the double dunk, remember? Hold on, you say, this is just the first night—as fire swoops through your insides. Walk around, gasp. Then suddenly bend forward and fall to your knees again. All night you pace, fall down, gasp like this, and twist up your face as if that that will keep you from dying. Against this are the scenes you try to hold in your mind. You're running onto the court for opening warm- ups and stuff the ball suddenly, turning a simple lay-up into a spectacular dunk. Whole gym is about to go beserk, but another series of stabs trickles through your stomach and spins your body in a circle. In one of these spins, you open your eyes long enough to notice that the shadows of the cell bars are gone. Daybreak has come. You've spent your first night in the Tombs, cold turkey. Wipe the tears from your face before the guard comes by to cheek. Sit on the floor, your back against the wall, staring at your toes. Maybe until tomorrow, you think, maybe until tomorrow, but you can't possibly last a week. Trying to pull a scene from the past doesn't work. You try to see yourself dunking the ball against somebody tall, Jackson or Kareern or Harper, but the players fade away from your screen and you're lying on the floor again kicking. And then you're focusing on the shadows of the cell bars, except they aren't there and now you know another day has passed. You want to get out of here and breathe easily for just a minute, just a tiny minute. Please, just a minute. You know it's no good, you can't last, so tell them to let you out. No, you can't give up, despite the fading scene of you dunking the ball, you strain to keep it in your mind.

No food or drink. You can't hold it. Every time you taste something it comes back to your mouth. Others are spitting up on you and moaning all night, right next to you. They've transferred you to another cell. You don't know when. Coughs, moans, shouts of let me out. Heads bang against the cement wall. Bodies pace around you as they go nowhere farther than the next corner. Food sits in plates—nobody can eat. Their bodies are propped up against the wall, mouths hanging open. One dude hanged himself last night, you remember hearing through the whirlwind of haze. If you can just get up high enough to dunk the ball, nobody can stop you. Three days, four days, a week. How many times an hour do you think of begging them to let you out? Didn't that little short dude who came in trembling fall on his knees crying and begging, praying to the guard to let him out? Cat lasted four hours. "Fuck this shit, I need me some smack," he said, leaving the cell without turning to look at you. Others growl, moan, go back to biting on their shoes or stuffing their shirts in their mouths to keep from crying. You step over the bodies to get to the toilet, the collection of people lying on the floor and gasping for relief. Why? How did you get caught up in this? What went wrong? Is it something you did? A feeling you had? These aren't people, just bodies removed from the gallery to come here to rot. Half of them won't stay a day because the shit's too heavy. Don't even mention something like three days.

One week. Chills every night. You shiver to a rhythm, knees knocking against each other. Once somebody—they're only faces, no names since nobody wants to know anybody—starts squealing and the strange whine starts you crying about nothing in particular and yet everything. Wiping your eyes, you feel the growing roughness on your cheeks. Could use a shower, too. But why? For somebody to spit up on you again? Keep your eye on the dunk shot out there, that's all. You get through one week and the second is easy as pie.

And then you're thinking that one day and look up to remind yourself that you have spent two weeks. It's light weight now. The dude in the gray pleated pants who keeps kicking you at night lies there moaning. A roach explores his forehead. By now the cell must have about a dozen dudes promising themselves at different times of the day and night that they are here to kick the shit. Many leave bent over and coughing after a day or two, while you keep your mind on the dunk shot you are about to make in a junior high school game. You are surprised at how you've withstood. Two weeks. No matter the stabs in your stomach, the empty, light feeling of the weight you have lost. Looking down at your body you see the saddest, thinnest legs and arms. Still, nothing will stay in your stomach. But you have no appetite anyway. Haven't eaten in sixteen days. Sixteen days. Then seventeen. Then eighteen.

Stand up with the craziest feeling. Step over the legs and chests of various addicts. Blink your eyes, stretch, then stand still and listen. Your stomach isn't growling, isn't even in pain. Clearing your throat, you sense something about your voice— it's, coming back? You frown, afraid to jump to conclusions. Listen. Walk around. No pains. No pains, Goat! You want to smile. Start giggling. Take a deep breath. No pains. Pat your stomach with your hand. No pains. Laughing now, you walk toward the cell door. In your mind, you are going up against Val and Vaughan at the Rucker and are about to slam it through. This is better than being high. When's the last time you felt this way? Take another deep breath. Take many. "I'm ready to leave." Cats on the floor look at you from the deep dozes which keep them down there. Louder, you repeat, "I'm leaving." Then you shout out to the guard that you want to get out. Already you're framing stories to tell to the fellows on the block. How cramped-up the cell was, how cats sprawled over the floor to sleep and get sick, screaming for their mammas, throwing up, frozen in bent-over positions from stomach pains. Roaches skirting over the shit just thrown up. And ages later you walk out clean. Oh, Goat, how did you do this? How did you save yourself from sure enough destruction? How did you break the back of the bitch? You want to throw back your head and chuckle. Damn, if your moms could see you now. If Yvette were here. Goat, there is a new life for you. You are no longer a part of these lost souls lying at your feet. You will never again in your life try to ruin your life. You really kicked ass this time, really. Shout out for the guard. You want out of here. You really did it. "Hey, I'm ready to get out of here!"

17

"We've been waiting for you, Goat." Four dudes sit at the long table in front of you. All have T-shirts with "Property of Greenhaven State Prison" across the front. You're still not accustomed to breathing freely, to seeing clearly, since you spent eighteen days in the Tombs. Six months now. Your whole body feels better. Even your voice is coming back.

"For what?"

"You know what." They're not smiling. You remember the cat on the end. He's been sent up for armed robbery. Never did speak too much. Lived in the East Bronx, you think.

"I don't know what. I don't know what you're talking about. I just got here last summer. I'm on the Rockefeller for five years." Five years. You just kicked the habit in the only way you can and be sure you won't go back, and they put your ass in prison for five years with a chance for parole in twelve months. If you kicked the habit, why you gotta go to this rehabilitation program? You already rehabilitated.

"Hey, did you really do cold turkey? I ain't never heard of nobody doing that shit—you Oscar?" The dark-skinned brother at the other end speaks.

Nodding your head, "Yeah. I did it."

This guy who's the leader, from the Bronx, is drumming his fingers on the table. "You know what you gotta do, Goat."

Feeling your temples get warm, you force out a half-sigh, half-laugh. "I don't know," holding out your hands.

"Tell him, Oscar."

"You gotta play ball, that's all. We heard through the grapevine that you weren't. Why?"

"I'm trying to forget it!" Look out the window. "I just want to forget about it for awhile. It don't feel good."

"Hey, man, you'd be really helping us. The league would get a lot of respect." He's leaning forward, eyes earnest.

But you're tired of ball now. You need to think about the rest of your life. It obviously ain't basketball that's going to do it. You already ruined the strength you had. You know what's happening. Alcindor going to Milwaukee, Bobby Hunter with the Globetrotters, the Hawk out at Phoenix. You, the Goat, in a drug rehab program, in prison. Upstate New York. Sent upstate is what the dudes used to say in junior high. Cats who came back wore processes and were "good," could whip anybody with their hands. They'd sit in the back of the room and doze. Teacher never woke them. Here's one from the Bronx now—probably never stayed awake for one class. And he's asking you how you kicked the habit. No, you don't want to play no ball. Just a whole lot of memories of what you could have been. Half of the million-and-half Lew is getting is how much? Plenty of money, you know that much. "Aw," standing up, your hands pushed into your pockets, "I ain't got it in me to play. I came here to rest and think, you know. Cool out."

"Goat, everybody from Harlem heard about you. You scored fifty-two against Watley, right? You did the double throwdown, the three-sixty. You stuffed the ball against the baddest, and would pin the pill against the backboard if they tried the shit on you. You dunked from the foul line, swooping through the air. I saw you against Val Reed and Vaughan Harper that day. You didn't know I was there. I threw a chair on the court. Hey, man, we need you to play. It would mean a lot for the program—your name and all."

What is this? Stand looking down on the exercise yard. What is he trying to do? You just got here three, four days ago, and they making demands already. You don't want to play. It'll just remind you of what you could have done. You're 25 years old, one of the best in New York, and what—you're in prison. You blew it. What can you say? So why torture yourself. You see Willis and Bradley down at Madison Square and think you should be out there. So you don't even watch them on television. It's too much torture. Cats in the pros make a move that sends the crowd into fits and it's a move you did in high school.

"Why won't you play, Goat?"

"I ain't got it."

"You'll always have it, brother. You just feeling sorry for yourself. You got the talent. Help us with the program, that's all we asking."

"Some people thought I was the best player in the city." Turning, you face the four at the table. "I had seventy-three college offers. I played with Lew and the Hawk. Now, I'm nobody, ex-addict and thief. I don't want to play. It'll just remind me of what I could have done, you know."

"Then you haven't learned anything," says the dude from the Bronx. "You ain't caught on yet, blood? Don't you realize why we're here?" he said, spreading his arms to include the other three. "Cause there's always hope, man. When I get out this muhfukah, I'm gonna make a million dollars in the clothing business. I know I can do it. I ain't giving up. That's what Chuck wants us to do—give up. Enough of us give up, he got us beat."

The others nod their heads, grunt. He's making sense. Pull out your chair and sit back down.

"All right you might not be able to play pro ball. But ain't no telling what might happen. You might run a scholarship program or a school or become a coach. You kicked the habit, didn't you? Then you can do anything, homeboy. You got your health, ain't you? Maybe it wasn't in the cards for you. You don't know. But ain't no sense in lying down and giving up, my man. No sense at all. You got a woman?"

"Yep."

"Your moms alive?"

"Yeah."

"Then you got it made."

The four of them stare at you. This is supposed to be one of those free encounters, where you get two hours to rap with each other. The staff social worker then comes in and talks shit. It's spring, 1970. You're 25 and already you have lived a lifetime. And the play-offs are starting. You all supposed to rap about your experiences. Shit, the only way you can get these niggers off dope is to lock them up and throw away the key. This ain't no program anyway. It's jail. Rockefeller probably making money on it. How the hell can you cure addicts by talking to them and not giving them any medication? Well, you ain't stupid enough to blow it. Sit there in the group sessions every morning and answer silly questions. Was your family matriarchal? Did you miss a father image? Was poverty a factor? Keep nodding your head yes and agree with everything they say. What can you lose? And now these brothers talking shit about don't give up. This whole place is a trip. But the fellows might be making sense. Why not play? What harm could it do? Give you something to do with your time. Make them feel good. Might even make you feel good. Get out of the routine of waking at eight and dribbling in the yard by yourself before anybody else comes on the court. Oh sure, you had to go out there, soon's you heard there was a court. Only been here three days and you've spent six hours on the court. Then back into your cell. Stare at the walls. Lunch. Yard exercises again. Some light games starting at three, then back into your cell. Rap session before dinner and another after dinner. Lights out at ten. Yeah, sure, get away from that dull shit. Hell, the brothers want you to. Go on. Play.

"Okay, okay," throwing up your hands to silence their rising voices. "Okay, I'll play," you say, then find a smile on your face as the brothers rise and walk out shaking your hand.

You have no idea that the news means so much. The next day, as you're warming some canned black-eyed peas and corned beef in a pot of boiling water, a dude comes up to you. Pretty soon he's telling you about the double dunk. "You're way ahead of your time, brother," he says. "Sure glad you're coming out for the league."

Damn, you're out of shape, body's fucked-up at twenty-five. But they stay on your back. Some brother from the city gets you in a group and reminds them who you are. "You know this brother's bad. He's one of the few who has 'the' before his name: The Goat. You got *the* Big O and *the* Pearl and *the* Hawk. Very few dudes get that, you know."

It takes the whole spring for you to get in half-way decent shape, before you can play the lightweight two-on-two's and three-on-three's, astonishing them with a few quick moves or skys, but not pushing yourself. One day in a full court run, five-on-five, you glance over to the side of the yard. Everybody in the damn prison is standing and watching. "They have heard you were playing," says one of your teammates as you run to set up. Even the guards are standing around.

Fuck it. Give them all you can. You have the courage to try something you haven't tried since you returned from Johnson C. Smith: the double dunk. You go up on a man and are in the air before he knows it and you are feeling good to have leaped this high without your heart thumping, and then you are slamming it down and catching it and slamming it down. Dance a few steps, turn, float in outer space for another few steps as the rhythm of the move takes over and envelops you. The walls of the prison reverberate with the yells of the inmates. You see them jumping up and down and slapping each other's backs. The fellows you're playing with just stop and drop their lower lips the way the guys used to do in the city. Five or six stop running to come over and shake your hand. The game is stopped for ten minutes.

Ten minutes is a long time to stand in an enclosed yard and listen to and look at people clapping for something you did. You remember seeing a television show about Lou Gehrig of the Yankees and how everybody in the stadium stood up to applaud the day he said he was retiring. This is how he must have felt. All the way up here in prison, in Greenhaven, New York, where they can watch the Knicks battle the Lakers for the championship and see Elgin go against Debusschere, Wilt against Reed, Jerry West against Clyde—and they're telling you here, Goat, that they appreciate you just as well.

You can always get a person to be on your side, support you. Even the militant brother from Brooklyn who talks mucho shit about revolution in basketball respects your views.

"Have you ever considered how silly you look, a grown man, running around in short pants and throwing up a ball?"

"Nope." Well, you haven't.

"Well, you know it's silly looking, right?"

"Yep."

"So why do you do it, Goat?"

"Cause I do it good."

"Yeah, that makes sense, brother. But you know the shit is exploitation, Goat. They're just exploiting your ass. They put you in funny looking uniforms and have you doing acrobatics like the Romans had their gladiators. Except here there's big bucks involved—television commercials, seats, tickets, stadiums, championships, all-stars—all that shit."

"So what's wrong with that?"

"Well, come on Goat, who are the players? I mean, who are seventy percent of the players? They're brothers, aren't they? Don't the brothers dominate the game as players? Now ask yourself who the owners are. Who owns the stadiums and the teams and the television stations and the seats and tickets and every fucking thing else? The white people! Now, when you guys get together to buy a team, then we'll have a revolution. But don't talk to me about revolutionary nationalism until then, brother." His face is red this afternoon in one of the rap rooms.

"Look here, man, I didn't talk to you about that shit anyway. You started it. I just happen to be in the room." Both of you laugh.

What he says about Kareem gets you to thinking. You still forget he's not Alcindor anymore, but a Muslim now—Kareem Abdul Jabbar. Wendell says that Kareem is the only revolutionary athlete: that he, after all the others talked big shit but finally copped out, was the only brother brave enough to boycott the 1968 Olympics. "The brothers had voted to boycott. Then they changed their minds and said let's participate but not accept medals. Then they changed to armbands and gloved fists to whatever you want to do." By this time his voice is raised. "Goat, I tell you Kareem is the only revolutionary we have. Those other jive suckers . . ."

Run, shoot, run all that summer. Run, shoot, run, shoot. You can feel yourself floating that extra second as you leap high again. Your touch is coming back, your quick step that lets you drive past a man in an instant. You can swat the ball away, leap from the foul line, fire from the side. You can play again. If nothing else, you can play again. Maybe next summer you'll be out on the courts of Harlem.

The inmates would sure like to see that. They'd like to see you doing it against the stars of Harlem and Brooklyn and maybe a few dudes from the Baker in Philadelphia and a few from the Newark league. You haven't been abandoned, Goat. They love you here, too. Another day you're warming another can of black-eyed peas in another pot of boiling water when a dude comes up to you. Pretty soon he's telling you about the double dunk. About fifty-two points against Watley. You're embarrassed. Dunking the ball over giants. He knows.

And so you don't feel so bad when they hip you to what's happening in the playoffs. Big Willis scores 38 in the first game. Big Willis against Big Wilt. Dudes are terrible. But you don't want to watch. You'd have to look at Elgin and Jerry West and McMillan and Bradley. You've seen them on the courts. Bradley even gave you some sneaks two summers ago. Now they on television. You listen to the end of the second game—stumbled on it as you enter the rap room—and hear about Jerry West making some incredible shot from near halfcourt. That's the kind of shot *you're* supposed to make. Game goes into overtime. But Willis gets 38 again and New York is happy as they take a two-game lead. Then you hear that Willis is injured in the fifth game—dropped to the floor with eight minutes to go. Wilt will destroy the Knicks, you believe. When Oscar runs down to tell you the Knicks took it anyway, you almost choke. Now Wilt goes wild, throwing in 45 points and grabbing 27 rebounds, and it's all left to the last game. "Who do you like, Goat?"

"I'm New York all the way, got to be," you say, but know you can't watch it on television.

"This is what I was talking about," says the brother from the Bronx. He tells you how Reed played his heart out in spite of his injury, then had to leave at half-time. Fourteen-point lead, though. "You can't ever give up. If shit don't go right, try another way, another angle. That's what it's all about, Goat. You can't stop playing ball because you didn't make it to the pros. Take a minute and check out what went wrong. You know what went wrong?"

"Uh, yeah."

"You sure?"

"No discipline. Spoiled. I couldn't do it."

"Yeah, that's it. The family broke down too, though. That's why we so far behind, Goat. We don't have that family strength. We need fathers and mothers raising our children, not just one or the other. If you had an old man who threatened to whip your black ass, you wouldn't be here today. You ain't never had no discipline, no male figure to straighten you out. Moms are usually cake. They give you what you want. I know what I'm talking about, brother. All this shit is clear to me because I've sat and thought about it. Show me a fucked-up nigger and I'll show you a fucked-up family."

Oh, yeah. Everybody has a game once they get in the Haven. Dumbest motherfuckers are suddenly worldly philosophers. Muslims know shit about the beginning of the world. Criminals from the Bronx know about family structure. High school dropouts can lecture on politics. You listen to it all and try to apply it to your own life. Finally, though, the reality is that you ain't in Madison Square Garden. Don't mean too much if you're a loser. Don't mean shit if your family was to blame. Don't mean doodley squat if it's all white folks. What you know is this: you were the best, shit went wrong, you blew. Now you're a reformed dope addict. Can't nothing make up for not being in the Garden. That organ, the packed stands, the shout, *"De-fense, de-fense, de-fense."* You won't hear it, and that's all that counts. They can keep the explanations. Bad breaks is how you explain it.

18

They're talking about dudes who weren't around a few years ago. Pete Maravich, Artis Gilmore—they all signed for big bucks recently. Sometimes you have to squinch your eyes and shake your head to keep from thinking about it. How you should be in the pros by now, pulling in that long bread. Well, sitting on the bench in Morningside, you think simply that you blew, Goat. Ain't no two ways about it: you blew. They're discussing Pistol Pete's passing, then go on to talk about the Pearl's passing, the Big O's passing, Jerry West's passing. One dude announces that Guy Rodgers made the pass to Wilt when he scored 100 points against the Knicks. Vote goes to the Big O. Ah, shit, you don't want to hear any more of this. Bad enough people keep asking you how you doing, meaning are you still on the shit. Then you got to hear about the world you are not a part of because you blew. Get up from the bench and slide toward the sidewalk.

"What's it look like, Goat?" Before you get a half block, you run into Snake.

"Ain't nothin' to it." Your heart slips down to your sneaks. He tips beside you. His dashiki is bright green.

"You see 'Like It Is,' the other day? Had some bad black poetry on there. Them brothers was gettin' down."

"Naw, me and Yvette looking for a pad."

"That right? How long you been back?"

"Two weeks. Seems like longer."

"You meet a brother named Ricardo in the Haven? Up for rape. Short dude with wide Afro?"

"Don't think so. I was in a special section."

"Had a teeny weeny mustache. Which way you headed?"

"Just walking, you know."

"What kind of place you looking for?"

"One bedroom. Darrin be staying with his granny 'til I can get a gig. One bedroom be enough."

"Dig, I'll definitely keep a lookout for you, bro. Watch out for that truck, motherfucker driving like he lost his mind. Goat, slide over to Nance's with me for a sec. Ain't nobody know you in town, be good to get together with you."

Lumps and rocks float in your stomach. The place where danger awaits you. You've been waiting for this since you got back. A flashing wish at night to get off would hit you for an instant, then dissolve. People have been looking at you strangely anyway since you got back and you insist on telling them you're off the shit. Now, the test. "Yeah, I can dig it."

His hand is on your arm now. He leads you across the street. Hey, hey to people on the corner, on stoops, in parked cars, in the doors of storefronts, hanging out windows. Imagine what they must be saying. That jive nigger still on the shit. Don't they ever learn? Why he waste his time like that?

"Oh, Goat"—tapping you in the side with his fist as you pass a record store—"just ran into an old friend of yours, Didn't you used to go with that Puerto Rican chick, uh . . ."

"Carmen?"

"Right. Well, she's a lawyer, man. I saw her downtown with one of those briefcases. She's an attorney with the attorney general's office. Ain't that a blip? She was always heavy, wasn't she?"

"Bet."

"Nance done got him a new crib. Stereo and shit. Wall-to-wall, great big color TV. He be glad to see you."

Dirty brown water trickles along the gutter. Kids on bikes zip between cars, dudes lean against posts as they rap to their mammas. You'd like to see the old addicts, see if they have learned anything about what they are doing to themselves. Why the fuck not? Good test, Goat, good damn test.

Into the lobby, up the elevator where the carpeted floor leads to the last apartment on the left. Chain lock bares one inch of facial exposure: "Yo?"

"Came by to see Nance. His man is here."

Door opens, air conditioning crawls up your arms, Sly and the Family Stone's bass beat bounces off the carpeting. Usual shit, you think, checking out the bodies laid out on the floor. One kid looks like a teenager, three women, the rest of them dudes. Here comes Nance, lifting himself up from his crouch and pushing aside his works. His smile is big, his hand is out.

"Goat, Goat. What it is? Heard you had come back, bro. You right on time, right on time. Cop a squat."

Sit in front of the television. The heads nod. Needles and plastic bags and caps and all the other shit are on the cocktail table. Everybody is mellow. You know exactly how mellow they are. You know how softly the clouds bounce off the forehead, how the world stops for you, how the eyelids weigh heavily. How many times a day, a week, a month, a year have you sat with the top of your head swirling above you, your mind focused on what is nothing more than the beginnings of dreams. This is the soft belly of your mommagran here, waiting for you to burrow your face against it. If you do, Goat, you won't have to worry any more about not making it to the pros. No, you can just burrow and hold on, the soft, warm belly rocking you into protective sleep. Clouds that make you forget.

"Goat?"

Everybody has stirred now into wakefulness. Legs cross, shoulders shake, eyes blink. Nance stands above you. Strangely, a flash of conversation you had with Carmen years ago, on your way to a hooky party, passes through your mind. Nance's eyebrows are raised. In his hand are the promises of soft clouds. His hand is out toward you, Goat. You may dream and float and forget if you wish. Your mommagran's belly is only seconds away.

"Yo."

"You wanna get down?"

"Naw, man, I'm off that shit." Force out a laugh. "I did cold turkey last year in the Tombs for eighteen days. Then I went to the Haven for over a year. I'm off that shit, man. I just came to say hello. Knock yourself out."

His face turns color and the muscles sag. You feel sorry for him because he's so embarrassed. He's standing there stunned.

"You beat heroin, Goat?" He's still standing. Snake is behind him.

"Yep. I couldn't eat or drink for a week. The pains, they were so bad, I couldn't do nothing but stay crouched up in a corner. I threw up every day and moaned and cried, but I didn't want to give up. I kept thinking about some of the things I did on the court—to keep from feeling the pains. It was some terrible shit, Nance, but I'll never use that fucking heroin again. It's an asskicker. It's a pimp. It don't care about your ass, it just wants your ass."

"I know, Goat. It takes you for a ride and drops you. But I can't . . ."

"I'm gon' get some water," rising, you say, "then get my hat." Grab his arm. "I really just came by to say hello, you know. I'm gonna split."

"Hey, you ain't got to rush, you know."

But you know he realizes after he says it that there is no reason for you to stay here. You ain't no dope addict. Besides, it's violation of parole to be in a place that has narcotics. Get your ass out of here. Shake their hands, go back to grab some cold water, regards to everybody, get out.

Downstairs in front of the building, you sigh. First big test. No sweat. You'll never go back. You start smiling. You'll never go back. You've kicked the habit for good, Goat. The world is yours now. Nothing can keep you from moving ahead. Walk up the street as you have never before, tipping, feeling good, real good. Hey, everything's cool. Wait until Yvette and Mom hear about this. They'll really smile.

This is the best summer you've had for a while and it's still early June. Play some ball, greet all the fellows returning from college. Tell the horror story of how you kicked the habit to all who stop to listen, whether it be in the playground, in the bar, or in somebody's store. Discussions of how strong the Knicks will be next year take place in all the playgrounds. Rudy stops one day to show everybody an article about you in the *Post*. How you were one of the best in the city. How you became a criminal and dope addict. How you kicked the habit. Rudy's reading the article as he stands on the foul line. You're too embarrassed to stay and use the moment to get some water.

Thanks to playing in prison, you're not out of shape totally, and can still excite a crowd, as Motorman would say, with a slam shot starting from the foul line. You've returned to your world. A man temporarily lost has found his way back. They still turn out to see the Goat play. You can pack a stadium. The Rucker pros have to let you play in that league—you're too good for the college league. "The Goat's back," yells a kid in the tree as you walk a dude baseline and line-drive the ball over your head so fast he doesn't even put up his hands. "The Goat's definitely back," yells a dude behind the basket as you do the three-sixty shot and tip it in backwards. "Show the pros something!" squeaks a woman holding her baby.

And that's the only kicker. You didn't go pro. All right, you may have kicked the habit, but that just leaves you free to do nothing. What to do with yourself. You didn't go pro. Behind the many greetings and compliments this first summer back are feelings of too bad because you didn't make the big time. It's too late now. You don't have that college degree. Even if you could get a special tryout, as some of your friends insist you should try for, you're sure you're out of shape. So what will you do with yourself? Yvette and you consider that question many, many times, and it always comes back to the same ol', same ol' thing: get a job. Before you can think seriously about how great it is to be back and how nice it would be to have gone on to the pros, you need a gig to sustain you. Sure, Van and Mister Burns and a half-dozen other pushers, gamblers and pimps give you spending cash when you run into them on the street. And you can borrow money any time. "You plan on doing this for the rest of your life?" asks Yvette. And the whole world suddenly looks immensely complicated. You don't have any skills, don't know anything or anybody having to do with anything else but basketball. Didn't learn shit in high school or college, don't have a degree. What can you do?

A hero with nothing but a legend behind you, that's what it turns out to be, Goat. There's still pain, right? Even the article written about you in the *Daily News* makes you flinch. You're back on the scene, the story says, still a hero, still trailed by little boys as you trek up and down the streets of Harlem. But then the story reviews what you've been through, what you could have become—*could* have become—and you poke out your mouth. It's always what you could have become that takes away from whatever glory you enjoy at the moment.

Then, on an overcast day in St. Nicholas Park as you watch some high schoolers run a three-on-three, somebody says something about how another basketball league is needed, especially one for younger players. You blink your eyes and frown in thought—consider that another league would be worthwhile. You could get the kids just by walking through the streets and putting up signs. Word of mouth. Everybody knows the Goat. You could call it the Goat tournament, with sweatshirts saying just that. Night games, referees, score table—real professional. Start smiling. Damn good idea. Stand and turn, looking for Rudy.

He's by the fence. When you walk up to him and Bob, you catch the last strands of a conversation about Wilt and Reed and how terrible they battled during the playoffs. Rudy is pushing his hip against Bob to demonstrate Reed's muscle.

"Hey," grabbing Rudy, "this is important. I was thinking about trying to start another basketball tournament during the summer. Call it the Goat tournament. I think it could work."

Both Rudy and Bob smile. You know they're with you. But then Bob asks you where you gon' get the bread.

Off the top of your head, you answer, "From the pushers. I know them all. They know me. They ought to do something for the community—they taking all the money out of it. I think I can get them to help."

"You'll need about five grand, Goat," says Rudy. "You might be able to get it by next summer. It's too late for this year, but sounds like a bet for next summer, Goat."

Yes, yes, yes. You'll be back in business. Doing your thing with kids. Real official like. You know how to explain it, too, so the pimps and pushers and all the underground brothers and sisters will want to contribute. Later that day, when you mention it to Van, he smiles, throws back his head and nods yes. "Damn good idea, ain't it, Beatrice?" The sister with heavy makeup sitting in the air-conditioned hog, her eyes red from smoke, agrees with Van. "Yeah, put me down for five hundred, Goat. But it'll have to be cash, you know what I mean? No checks, man, just cash. You know I'm good, check with me next spring, bro. Hey, you seen Scottie lately?"

In poolrooms, in alleys. In shooting galleries, on corners. Bars, restaurants, record shops. All summer you scrounge around, searching out the many who earn their money under the table. Nobody can say no to the Goat. Some pout and sigh, but only for a moment. When they hear who else is putting up bread they come around. "Sure, Goat. You kicked the habit. You deserve to get your shit off."

Yvette is not at home when you go to tell her that in three weeks you have raised five thousand dollars from dope pushers, numbers backers and pimps. They've all guaranteed you the money for next summer. There will be a Goat Tournament, a Harlem summer basketball league organized by the star who turned junkie and then came back. You're standing at her front door, out of breath from having run through the July streets, ready to grab her and tell her the good news when the door opens and her father's bald head shines in your face. You two have always been just cool. He threatened to kill you two years ago. Now you speak and go about your business, he goes about his. You know what he's thinking: you're an ex-addict with no job and running the streets in sneaks and a sweatshirt while his daughter, Yvette, is out looking for an apartment. You aren't worth the time of her day. He's never said two words to you, which means you have to guess what he's thinking. If he would only say something.

"I saw that article about you." He's turned his short body and walks toward the couch. You guess you should follow him. "Want some iced tea?" Eyes blaze. The muscles in his arms flinch as he turns toward the kitchen. He mumbles something while the refrigerator door is open and you can't hear him. "I said, did you really kick the habit like the newspaper says?" He's peeking around the door of the refrigerator at you.

"Yes sir. I'm having a basketball tournament, too, next summer. I raised five grand."

He stands at the doorway of the kitchen with the two glasses of iced tea, the lemons floating. Shaking his head, he says nothing, hands you a glass, nods for you to sit. The cushions go whoof when he sits next to you.

"I think you're a loser, Earl Manigault." His eyes blaze, he's breathing heavy and staring right at you. "But you've managed to kick the worst habit in the world. Don't ask me how, since you've never acted responsibly, don't know what discipline is and aren't much more than a spoiled bum. But somehow you've managed to...recover something of your manhood. I was impressed by that newspaper article. I wanna shake your hand and tell you that you could prove me wrong about being a loser. You might."

19

"Who's this?"

One of the young dudes with his hands stuffed in his pockets and an Afro comb sticking in his hair is on his toes peeking out the storefront window.

"Aw, try that shit with somebody your own age, young boy," you say.

"Hey, I ain't kiddin', man. There's a black limousine out there and a little white man is getting out. He got a chauffeur, too."

Here it is the winter after your first summer out the Haven and you're shivering in a storefront on Seventh and One-Seventeen, shooting the bull with the dudes in the Street Academy. You've gotten promises from enough people to make sure you'll get your tournament started next year. Plus you've given a few speeches at schools and churches and recreation areas about the dangers of narcotics. You like standing in front of these kids and telling them what it was really like. Their eyes boggle when you describe cold turkey and shooting galleries and cramps in your stomach. You wouldn't wish your luck on a dog, and you tell them just that. "Dope ain't no good for you," you tell them, looking solemn. Now stand in the academy, where you've been working as a counselor since August, thanks to Mr. Blakley, fairly happy now that you and Yvette have your own apartment and your life looks good. Some guy, Axthelm, has written a chapter on you in his basketball book. You're still a hero. Things are going well—no hassles, no big problems. And wait until the summer. And plenty of fun like this dude's jiving.

"Right, and he's throwing away one-hundred dollar bills, too—huh, Victor?"

The voice at the door startles all of you: "I'm looking for Earl Manigault." Nobody says a thing. Dark suit standing there as if he owns the place. Hell, you clean, ain't got nothing to hide, walk forward.

"I'm Earl Manigault."

He strides over to you and takes your hand. "I'm Bill Daniels. I own the Utah Stars. I read about you in that book, *The City Game.* Can we talk?" Feet shuffle. You can feel the glances directed by the dozen dudes sitting in chairs around the room.

He must be serious. No white man would come up here and try to pull this shit. He's too little anyway. Follow him out the door. Ain't nobody said a thing, including Victor. "Call the cops if I'm kidnapped." You smile.

Get in the back seat with him and a brother introduced to you as Ron Lyle, a heavyweight boxer. Daniels asks you if you're interesting in coming out to the Stars tryout camp in the summer. You're dazed. Glance at Ron Lyle. He shakes his head, meaning the dude's serious. For you, it's too much like Hollywood. Big limousine with chauffeur way up there in the front, glass windows between you, soft gray upholstery, rug on the floor. You're dazed, and find yourself nodding and agreeing as if you're high again and are seeing things through that familiar haze. Limousine takes off, your boys come running out the door to the sidewalk and you look out the back window to see them standing there with the strangest looks on their faces. You're off to the Nassau Coliseum where the Stars are playing the Knicks tonight. "I want you to meet the coach, Bill Sharman."

Daniels talks about your double dunk. His investment in cable television. Ron Lyle's future as the next heavyweight champion. What are you supposed to say? Is this what Miss Rosa meant when she read your palm for free at Christmas and predicted that a big car would change your future? Her head wrapped in a turban, the strange glass crystal ball glowing in the little room and her two kids who your moms claims are gypsies peeking out from behind the curtains—she almost scared you. "Do not walk on Broadway late at night. Watch out for the number seven. A woman named Carla will bring you good news."

Is somebody playing games with you or are you really sitting next to the owner of the Utah Stars way up here in his private box? Is this really coach Bill Sharman to whom the owner introduces you? Are you really in the locker room after the game and talking to forward Willie Wise? It's January and they're talking about next September and rookie camp and a tryout for you. Sharman says you're a guard although you think you could play forward. But the competition. The Stars won the ABA championship last year. They've got three great guards already—Marv Jackson, Ron Boone and Glen Coombs. Only one guard position remains for you and whoever else will be shooting for it. You'll have to work your ass off between now and September to get back in shape. They think you can do it. You think you can do it.

Much later that evening you're shaking hands goodbye with Bill Daniels. The dream continues. Even as the long, black limo slides up the avenue, you're not sure this is happening. Try now to reconstruct this day. You are in the Street Academy, Bill Daniels walks in from nowhere and asks for you, then drives you out to the Coliseum with Ron Lyle in the back seat with you. You meet the coach and the players and are then invited to the rookie tryout camp in September. All of this in a day. You had given up playing ball for real. Now you've got to get ready for a tryout. Who can you thank for all this? Who's responsible for this overtime period where you have the chance to go ahead and win? You sigh, smile and walk into your building. Yvette will think you're joking.

It's no joke, though. Winter hits the city harder than it's been hit in years. There is too much snow for you to run in the streets, so you work out in various gyms in Harlem and in the Bronx. Quick quarter-mile sprints, then jog around slowly followed by a high speed sprint, then a jog. Repet until your heart trips. Weights on your ankles to get your spring back. Push-ups and muscle-stretching exercises. Pull-ups. Sit-ups. The hurting pangs are easily ignored because you have one image stuck in your mind: playing for the Stars, in the big time finally, where you belong, despite all the shit you've gone through. You do 75 sit-ups and smile at the aches in your stomach. These aches are nothing compared to what you're used to. This winter as the Bucks with Alcindor and Robertson terrorize the NBA, you keep the image of playing finally with the big cats in your head. You can actually watch the playoffs in the spring and marvel at the still-fluid motion of an older Oscar Robertson playing with a maturing Alcindor. Better watch them—you may be against them next year. You may actually be playing—no, not *may* be; tell yourself you *will* be.

"Gettin' ready, huh Goat?" Everybody knows what's happening. People can tell you exactly what you said to Bill Daniels three months ago and what he was wearing when you said it. Word travels as it always does in Harlem—quickly, with embellishment—and not one person fails to wish you good luck, whether you're running through the streets or riding a bicycle.

Your heart refuses to slow down when summer comes and the Rucker Tournament begins. Three months from now you'll be down to the wire. You'll be out there for the real thing. The final big chance in your life. The last overtime.

The Rucker is bad as usual, with some new names on the lips of many. Motorman has moved out to the coast, somebody tells you, so the flamboyance is not quite there. Freddie Crawford and Bob McCullough are the new directors. Your man Charlie Scott of the Squires and Dean the Dream of the Knicks are the fast guards. The J—Julius Erving—takes off from the foul line and twists the ball in a small circle before he slams. Nobody's seen anything like that since the Hawk. They call him the Doctor. Still, your double dunk has not been matched by anybody, and when you explode with it, Eighth Avenue is in an uproar. You wait until a few seconds of quiet exists between the warmup shots, when the sudden hush of expectation fills the air as you take down a lay-up and dribble out to the foul line. And when those seconds are there—you can sense it—you leap forward and slam it through, grab it and slam it through again. "Ooh, the Goat!" yells a voice. Nobody else takes a shot for a good half-minute.

By August you know there is nothing else you can do. For eight months you've been getting yourself ready, and you can only get so ready. The night before you leave, you watch the sunset over the Hudson like the evening you and Mister Rucker watched it and he told you it is a shame to waste talent. You wish he could be here with you now to put his arm around your shoulder. Then you go back to the pad and sit with Yvette. Small talk is hard. What to say? Everybody in Harlem is counting on your ass. Your chest is tight. You won't be able to sleep, you realize that. Darrin sits with a ball on the floor, black and white slashes move soundlessly across the screen, and Aretha moans on WWRL. Finally you and Yvette fall asleep on the couch.

With an hour to get to the airport the next day, Mango, Bob, Ricardo and Pablo come to get you. Say goodbye quickly to Yvette and walk out with Pablo carrying your bags. Your palms are sweaty when you get in the car.

"Don't jump too much, Goat," Pablo says. "Oh yeah, Lew said to wish you good luck. But look, you'll be in the back court, so conserve your energy. You know, take it easy. Give it to the corner, cut, try to keep the pace and get your wind back."

Feel for your ticket and the six hundred dollars various friends have given you as you listen to their advice. Traffic is light. Park at the airport. Check in. Ready to boarding. Everything too fast, too clear—no blurriness, no haze. Your temples bang. Shake hands goodbye with everyone. Sincere good wishes. Then you are waving and walking backward toward the gate and getting on the plane.

Wouldn't you know it. The guy sitting next to you has read about your tryout. A thousand questions until you take a deep breath and tell him you want to take a nap. Damn. Leave you alone. Let you think a little bit, anyway.

But it's worse when you land. Who was it said it was a publicity stunt? Some brother from Lenox Terrace. Three, four newsmen talking at once while you wait for your bags. You've missed the assistant coach. One reporter mentions dope addiction. Three people around you freeze into a stare. Jump into a cab to the Travelodge. Your roommate, Floyd, is already there, unpacked, a smile and handshake to put you at ease. Call your moms and Yvette, look out the window at white mountains. They'll never get you to ski, you know that much. Heard somebody in the elevator talking about the helicopter from the roof. People are crazy. Give them some money and they'll do anything. Fourteen rookies and a few holdovers. Some tough odds. They can't take but one, *maybe* two.

At dinner you are interviewed by the local television station. You are the celebrity, the favorite rookie. Are you in shape? Are you as good as professional players? Are you using drugs now? Do you wake up in the morning with stomach pains? How many girlfriends do you have? Smile, wince, try to answer without going off. The first morning is a long time coming with ten-minute lay-up drills. Dribble the length of the court with your right hand, then back down with your left. This is the intellect working on pure, raw talent, according to Motorman. Harness the ghetto. Take your talent and try to make it seem inadequate. Divide into groups of three and play twenty-one. Twenty minutes of wind sprints. Now you go into fast break plays down the length of the court. Go to the foul line, shoot ten, shower, dress and ride back to the motel. Fall out, realizing you got evening practice too. Eight months of getting in shape and you're almost bushed?

Evening scrimmages are ass-kickers. Seven, eight hundred people fill the stands at Cottonwood High School. You go a full forty-eight minutes. One game you score sixteen points, but you don't have the feel, and tell those who come out of the stands after the scrimmages that you aren't at your best yet. The daily stories quote you. You're coming along. Miss your family.

EX-ADDICT TRIES TO MAKE IT.
JUNKIE WINS NEW DAY ON COURT.
DOUBLE DUNK HASN'T BEEN SEEN YET.
IS MANIGAULT NERVOUS?

Every day a new feature full of questions.

But never more than 16 points. Only four in one game—the lowest you've ever scored in your life. Shots go around the rim and come out. Instead of dunking the ball, you play the safe lay-up. Don't know why you won't dunk. Done it on cats much taller than these. They're not better than you. They're *not*. Maybe you're scared? Your man runs you into picks, and you're going so fast, the impact against the six-ten center dazes you as your man escapes and lays it up.

"You've got a team out there," says the coach. "You can't do it all. Give the ball up more to the big man."

Yeah, that's fine, but everybody's out here for himself and that seventeen-thousand-dollar contract. A few signs like, "We're with you Goat" encourage you, but you can't seem to get it together totally. Yvette's voice warns you not to give up. You could explode any day, soon's you relax more. She promises you'll loosen up.

Faces disappear as cuts are made. Ten are left. Then six. Then the coach calls you into his office after the last practice.

Walking up the stairs to his suite, you think about your tournament next year. Plus you been talking to Bob McCullough about opening up a sporting goods store. Look, you can't lie down and die. You've got two women who'll do anything to make you happy, a fine son, the fact that you did kick the habit. Other people are worse off than you.

He's busy filling out forms. Reminds you of Mister Shanker. He looks up, doesn't smile, puts out his hand for you to sit. Phone rings, he mumbles into it, then sits back with his hands behind his neck.

"We can't use you. This is a team game ... you try to do it all yourself ... your defense is hopeless... timing is off ..."

You know he's talking but you haven't heard anything but no. He said no. Your mind is back in Mt. Morris Park when you found the dude who had called the cops on you and said you had stolen his jacket. You found him in the park by himself, went over to the jive punk and punched the shit out of him for telling that lie. The sweet pain of your hand banging into his cheek. You could have killed him. Why'd he tell that crazy lie? Now you'd like to punch somebody just like that. Not the coach. Not any of the players. Not even the pussy newspaperman. Just somebody. Somebody. Somebody because he said no.

Blank. Everything is blank and red. Everything has dropped from your stomach and left it hollow. Your heart is burning. They can't use you, the inventor of the double dunk. Fifty-two against Watley. Timing off. No defense. Didn't you stop the baddest in Harlem? Right, right, right, right. Sure. Why bother. Hell. Go to the shower. Don't talk to anybody.

A writer from *Sports Illustrated* insists. Okay. He kept four of the six. You didn't make the last four. No. you haven't any hard feelings, just sadness. You are a blank again. The greatest thing in the world for you just slipped away. You can't scream or cry or kick or bang. A blank. Back in your room, you call Yvette with a shaky voice. Beat around the bush, ask about the weather, how she feeling and jive like that. She interrupts to tell you she knows. She feels it in your voice. You're sorry, you did your best, you made the last cut and then you were out and you'll be back as soon as you talk to Bill Daniels. You're sorry, you did your best.

"Come on home, Earl," Yvette says. "Come on home."

You stay two more days until Bill Daniels arrives. He looks up at the ceiling of your room.

"What job would you like, Earl?"

"I'd like to play."

"What job would you like outside of playing?"

"I'd like to finish my education."

"Do you have any specific school in mind? If not, I know a school out here that I could get you into."

Yvette tells you to take it. You don't want to go back home now anyway. Sounds a little better to say you're in school out here. But you have no idea he means Snow College, one hundred and ten miles from Salt Lake City. And one hundred twenty-five white students. You're practically in prison again. White snow, white students, white music, white teachers. No varsity team, nobody to talk to. Prison in Utah. He means well, but you'll lose your mind. You don't care if it's a little hard, but this? Two weeks later you get your hat and book for Manhattan. Next summer your tournament will be in its second year. You'll talk to Bob about the sporting goods business. You may give some more talks at high schools. Look, you tell yourself, staring at the mountains over the wing, people are worse off than you. Sigh and close your eyes. See Kenny Bellinger leaping between the buildings.

LaVergne, TN USA
28 June 2010
187576LV00002B/159/P